CHARLES DICKENS
AS SERIAL
NOVELIST

Charles Dickens

AS SERIAL
NOVELIST

ARCHIBALD C. COOLIDGE JR.

THE IOWA STATE UNIVERSITY PRESS, AMES, IOWA, U.S.A.

ARCHIBALD C. COOLIDGE, JR. is associate professor of English at
the University of Iowa, Iowa City, where he teaches courses
surveying the history of the English novel. He was graduated
from Harvard in 1951 and holds a doctorate from Brown University. His writings include more than a dozen articles on
Dickens in specialized periodicals.

© 1967 The Iowa State University Press
Ames, Iowa, U.S.A. All rights reserved

Composed and printed by
The Iowa State University Press

FIRST EDITION, 1967

Library of Congress Catalog Card Number: 67–12135

TO LILLIAN

PREFACE

I HAVE DERIVED a general sense of the significance of what Dickens said and did from teaching courses in English literature and thought from 1700 to 1900, especially a history of the English novel. The book as a whole is the outgrowth of my discovery ten or twelve years ago that one vast cluster of Dickens's techniques was related to the fact that his novels were published serially. The details are the result of the collection of some 25,000 separate facts about Dickens's novels.

Where it has seemed relevant, I have indicated Dickens's relation to the history of the novel. Thus I have mentioned Carlyle briefly, have glanced at the impressionists, and have discussed Mrs. Radcliffe's work at some length. The discussions of the nature of the novel range more widely and are not limited to those authors closely connected to Dickens.

The backbone of the book is an original study

(copyrighted in 1956) of the relationship of serialization to the forms and techniques of Dickens's novels. Since I began my investigation, John Butt and Kathleen Tillotson have published a most interesting study of Dickens as a serial novelist and have produced a general awareness of the serialization of his fiction. I have found their book, *Dickens at Work* (1958) very stimulating. Working primarily in another direction, however, I am seeking to show what Dickens did in order to produce the magnificent unities of effect and meaning which Mr. Butt and Mrs. Tillotson quite rightly insist Dickens achieved despite his serial composition. Mr. Butt and Mrs. Tillotson broach the subject in their discussions of *David Copperfield* and *Dombey and Son*, but by and large they concentrate on other matters.

The data I have collected include many from previously unused sources, especially Dickens's discussions of his writing in his speeches and the articles he wrote about literary topics. There are, in addition, many important pieces of information in the hundreds of remarks about his work quoted in scattered passages in the biography by his friend John Forster. Only a few of the significant patterns in these remarks were noticed by Forster or have drawn the attention of twentieth-century scholars. I have explored these thoroughly and have drawn heavily also on my own observations of all of Dickens's fifteen novels. Hence I have been able to make a number of discoveries about the details of Dickens's procedure which are described in this book along with more broadly significant matters.

The following details of the argument are "firsts" or discoveries: (1) the description of the interchangeable stock characters used by Dickens; (2) the description of the installment patterns which are the basic units of Dickens's novels; (3) the discussion of Dickens's development as a symbolist; (4) the demonstration that Dickens used impressionism; (5) the explanation of the symbolic polarity in Dickens's plots; (6) the demonstration of Dickens's use of Mrs. Radcliffe's techniques for arousing constant curiosity and anxiety about an endangered protagonist; (7) the explanation of Dickens's increasing tendency to focus upon a maturing protagonist.

In addition to the debts indicated in my notes and acknowledgements, I should like to express my gratitude for the encouragement I have received in regard to this study or its parts from the following scholars of the novel or of the Victorian period: the late R. Gale Noyes, who directed my thesis, and the late George Wiley Sherburn; Leicester Bradner, Leslie Staples, William Buckler, Warrington Winters, and George Worth. I wish to thank the University of Iowa, which helped defray the expense of publication. I am grateful also to Mrs. Arlene Lehman, who has typed the recent drafts of this book. Most of all I must thank my wife who read and discussed Dickens with me and made many valuable criticisms and suggestions; who collected data on modern serials for me; and who typed at least four drafts of the book.

ACKNOWLEDGMENTS

I THANK the following publishers for permission to use materials previously printed:

Appleton-Century-Crofts, Division of Meredith Publishing Company, for permission to quote some lines from *The Nineteenth Century and After* by Samuel C. Chew. *A Literary History of England, Vol.*

4., edited by Albert C. Baugh, copyright, 1948, by Appleton-Century-Crofts, Inc. Reprinted by permission of Appleton-Century-Crofts, Division of Meredith Publishing Company.

Chapman and Hall Limited, for permission to use in Appendix 1 a collection of page numbers and dates indicating the installments in Dickens's serials. These materials are drawn from T. Hatton and S. Cleaver, *A Bibliography of the Periodical Works of Charles Dickens,* Chapman and Hall, London, 1933. The details of my use of this material are described in the notes to Appendix 1.

The Clarendon Press, Oxford, for permission to quote from Kathleen Tillotson, *Novels of the Eighteen-Forties,* the Clarendon Press, Oxford, 1956.

The editor of *The Dickensian,* for permission to quote from K. J. Fielding's review of *Dickens and the Twentieth Century* in *The Dickensian,* January, 1963.

Doubleday & Company, Inc., for permission to quote from Mr. Ley's notes in *The Life of Charles Dickens* by John Forster, edited by J. W. T. Ley, Doubleday & Company, New York, 1927.

Lawrence and Wishart, Ltd., for permission to quote from T. A. Jackson, *Charles Dickens, The Progress of a Radical,* Lawrence and Wishart, London, 1937.

The Modern Language Association of America, for permission to quote some lines from *PMLA.* These lines are reprinted, by permission of the Modern Language Association, from Fred W. Boege, "Point of View in Dickens," *PMLA,* LXV, No. 2 (March, 1950).

The editor of *The Modern Language Review,* for permission to quote from K. J. Fielding, "Charles Dickens and the Department of Practical Art," *The Modern Language Review,* XLVIII, No. 3 (July, 1953).

Oxford University Press (New York), for permission to quote from John Butt and Kathleen Tillotson, *Dickens at Work,* Essential Books, Fair Lawn, New Jersey, 1958.

Philosophical Library, Inc., for permission to quote from Jack Lindsay, *Charles Dickens, A Biographical and Critical Study,* Philosophical Library, Inc., New York, 1950.

Portions of Chapter 8 appeared first in a periodical. I wish to thank the editor of *The Dickensian* for permission to reprint, in this chapter, much of my article "Dickens's Complex Plots," *The Dickensian,* LVII, Autumn, 1961, and about half of my article "Charles Dickens and Mrs. Radcliffe: A Farewell to Wilkie Collins," *The Dickensian,* LVIII, Spring, 1962.

Portions of Chapter 11 appeared first in periodicals. I wish to thank the chairman of the editorial board of the *North Dakota Quarterly* for permission to reprint, in this chapter, my articles "Charles Dickens' Creation of Story from Character," *North Dakota Quarterly,* Vol. 31, Nos. 1 and 2, Winter-Spring, 1963, and "The Unremoved Thorn: A Study of Dickens' Narrative Methods," *North Dakota Quarterly,* Vol. 30, No. 1, Winter, 1962. I wish also to thank the editor of *The Dickensian* for permission to reprint, in this chapter, the remaining half of my article "Charles Dickens and Mrs. Radcliffe" described above. Finally, I wish to thank the business manager of *The Mississippi Quarterly* for permission to reprint, in this chapter, my article *"Great Expectations,* the Culmination of a Developing Art," *The Mississippi Quarterly,* XII, Fall, 1961.

ARCHIBALD C. COOLIDGE, JR.

CONTENTS

CHARLES DICKENS
AS SERIAL
NOVELIST

THE ARTISTIC
SIGNIFICANCE OF
SERIAL DISTORTION

CHARLES DICKENS created novels so brilliant that such distinguished writers as Shaw, Dostoyevsky, Tolstoy, and Kafka, called him their master. Dozens of other authors of note, four generations of novelists, have learned from his art. This international literary respect[1] and Dickens's continued popular appeal are the historical evidence that Dickens is one of the world's greatest literary artists. Even a small discovery about the art of such a man has several values at once. It is interesting by itself as a fact concerning an extraordinary human being. It casts light on great and still widely read books. It has significance as part of a continuing history of literary influence. It offers a clue to the universal nature of artistic creation itself. An original study of any broad aspect of his work becomes as much a new exploration of the fundamental art of fiction as an original study of Plato would become willy-nilly a new introduction to all western philosophy. This

3

book attempts to show that serial publication presented to Dickens in exaggerated form certain important
problems which are peculiar to the novel as a genre
and that he solved these problems magnificently. The
solutions help explain his being so interesting to other
novelists and the general public.

A book on such a subject must combine the kinds
of literary study most common today. The reason is
simple. A survey of the articles on novelists during
the years 1958–1960 in the forty leading English and
American literary periodicals shows that the most frequent type of essay explains how a certain theme or
symbol is to be found organizing one particular novel.
Critics in favor of such an organic approach tend to
decry other kinds of criticism as mechanical.[2] Dickens
himself used mechanical and organic views together.
Moreover, the general artistic significance of his struggle with serial publication lies in the way his vision
of the world enabled him to overcome difficulties, in his
brilliant organic shaping of solutions to common,
though little understood, mechanical problems. Any
book attempting to describe this subject then must
respect both kinds of approach and must take a cue
from Dickens's own ideas on the matter.

Dickens's awareness of these two aspects of his
art takes the form of what seems at first a paradoxical
idea of himself as an artist who was a prophet and a
carpenter. About *Our Mutual Friend* he wrote that
he saw it all and merely wrote it down as it was revealed to him.[3] In regard to *Oliver Twist* he expressed
the agonies he went through in writing the ending
because he considered the characters realities whose
lives he reported.[4] Part of the time, then, he saw
himself as a prophet to whom the world of his fiction
was revealed in existence. Yet he wrote Collins once
that to interest people in something bad a writer had

to picture a girl victimized by it.[5] He wrote about his work in *Dombey and Son* as a soup to which he was adding ingredients of character and plot.[6] In addition, in letters to many authors who were submitting manuscripts to his periodicals he advised them to be dramatic, vivid, etc.[7] In short, at other times, Dickens saw himself as the active constructor of literary devices to inject ideas into people's heads and to entertain. As the letter about showing something bad reveals, however, the construction and carpentry are included in the prophecy. Dickens knew he was a carpenter so he might be a prophet.

To be fair to a novelist with such a double view, a critic must find some way of fusing the two main trends in novel criticism. Nevertheless, as I have suggested, many of the best books on Dickens since 1935 have concentrated on the prophet. They have contained collections of articles or chapters exploring the use of this theme or that symbol.[8] Such discussions tend to emphasize Dickens's imaginative vision of life, and from them the public has gained a deep impression of this very important aspect of Dickens's art. These studies have described the organic unity of the individual novels. Their authors have had a firm grasp of Dickens's symbols and a sensitive reaction to his stories. They have been able to create the experience of reading a Dickens novel with a virtually simultaneous awareness of his finest shades of meaning and his careful shepherding of different details toward one great end. These critics have even tended to retell the story of a novel in the process of discussing it. Proceeding novel by novel they have also recaptured some of the vision and charm of the original. Retracing a great author's footsteps, they have seemed to praise each book to the skies and have emphasized the unity of a work as a fact because an imaginative world and a unified intention could be detected and described.

This criticism has explored only a portion of what Dickens considered his art. We must remember that Dickens was the greatest technical virtuoso and innovator in nineteenth-century fiction and that he believed variety and paradox were as important as unity. Much of the greatness of such an author can be seen only by mechanical analysis. It is not surprising then that there are some indications Dickens criticism for the last five years has been shifting toward the mechanical. K. J. Fielding in a review of a new collection of essays on Dickens, *Dickens and the Twentieth Century* in the January, 1963, *Dickensian,* says "critical consideration of character and plot is in favour again. The change has even gone so far that some of the present writers are cautious about stressing anything that has been said recently about Dickens's use of themes and symbols in the novels." This kind of discussion tends to be analytic and often, though not always, treats first this aspect, then that, of many novels at once. Because it treats parts of a work which can be built (and could in theory be built by any man), it omits the artist's vision. Hence, unfortunately, it tends to seem to reduce great art to a bag of cheap tricks and to emphasize imperfectly dovetailed details and incompletely executed intentions, thus denying perfect unity to most works.

The fusion of these two approaches is not really difficult. The symbolic criticism has always been much influenced by the organicist assumptions of its practitioners. They seem to feel that if a man has a sweeping imaginative picture of life it automatically reaches paper (or another medium) and automatically entrances its readers. Dickens's many remarks about constructing stories indicate that he, for one, did not believe in any such laborless transfer. The symbolic approach assumes that somehow an author has always known all the ways to write a story. Therefore, he is felt to have no problems to solve once he sees the grand prospect to be captured in this or that novel. Everything else is supposed to follow deductively. I suggest it would be more adult to recognize that writing a novel of four hundred to eight hundred pages is more like building a cathedral than jotting down the few notes of a simple melody which has come to mind as a unit. Such a vast undertaking must proceed from an imaginative and organically unified vision, but it requires much time and much work. It involves within its organic execution many mechanical problems and solutions in order that the stone and the colored glass may be put in the proper places. We must discover what the novelist sees in life, for mechanical devices by themselves do not make a good novel. We must also examine the author at work facing problems and gradually during his career developing ways of solving these problems.

What Dickens saw in life has been made somewhat familiar to us through the work of the symbolic critics mentioned above. Particularly in his later years, he had a tendency to regard the world as a prison of some kind. His main sympathy was with the semi-criminal trapped inside some system, parental, educational, legal, industrial, financial, tyrannical, environmental, or ecclesiastical. He would follow the fortunes and paint the absurd and terrifying experiences of the victims. He would picture the peculiar wolves who stalked through these institutional forests, using every trifle of social custom or conventional moral pressure to cover their advance. Then, with greater or lesser optimism, he would indicate that the way out into the sunlight lay in sympathy for other people. He would suggest ultimately that the mitigation of horror or the possibility of a new life was love.[9]

As for mechanical difficulties, he had one monumental problem, as the biographical evidence and the evidence of constant remarks in his letters show. This problem was the difficulty with structure arising from the disjointed publication of the serial. Each of his stories was first published as a serial. It was like trying to paint the Mona Lisa on a score of pieces of paper the size of postage stamps.

Essentially, serial plotting tempted Dickens, whatever his *unity* of imaginative vision, to give his stories only the crudest kind of structure. At times he gave in to this temptation. A hack would always have done so. But Dickens cared about his vision of life and apparently took the temptation as a challenge. He developed a highly sophisticated structural method in response to serial publication so that his novels might embody more and more of the world he saw. This challenge of the serial had three parts. Serial plotting encouraged the creation of a novel structure which had a kind of arrangement of its parts in space like a candy box packed with different sweets. It encouraged also a kind of arrangement in story time like the beads on a string. Finally, it encouraged the production of a story without connections between parts and with little thought about or development of any one part. The hostile criticism which Dickens's novels met at times, especially after 1850, shows that some people saw that in many of his novels in varying degrees Dickens succumbed to these temptations. Yet Dickens worked to civilize and overcome each of these serial tendencies. The sections of this book will show that Dickens succeeded because of his devotion to his vision. They will describe how that devotion enabled him to surmount the three parts of the serial challenge.

The three parts of the serial challenge are interesting merely as facts concerning a great writer and
as explanations of certain features of some of the most
widely read novels in English. Yet their broad implications make them much more important and suggest
why Dickens labored to deal with them. Each of the
temptations of the serial was a weird exaggeration of
a problem typical of the novel as a genre (hence as a
challenge met, of course, each was to some extent responsible for Dickens's greatness as a novelist). Every
novelist can find he has such a variety of events and
pictures to present that he thinks of descending to the
candy box kind of arrangement. Every novelist can
feel so strongly that his plot must advance now and
then that he is tempted to descend to an oversimple
arrangement of events like beads on string. Every
novelist can find his story or plot situation so complicated that he overlooks the matter of connecting and
developing the individual parts. It is true, to give in
thus is to betray his particular idea and general world-
view. The beginning novelist, however, may not be
able to solve these problems. The hack may not bother
to. The mature artist has learned solutions to them
(very often Dickens's) or has developed his own. He
uses the solutions without special self-consciousness
about what he may consider rather elementary matters.

Yet these problems and the kinds of solutions
Dickens and others have found for them derive from
the fact that the novel is a very special kind of story and
different from a play, an epic, a medieval romance, or
a short tale. To put it briefly, despite the frequent suggestion that only trivial mechanical differences in
presentation exist between stories in these genres, I
suggest that the novel is different from other kinds of
story in several basic ways. It uses vast masses of
familiar detail. In consequence, more than other genres

it presents to its author the problem of organizing a large body of forgettable but meaningful detail. Essentially the original novelist presents a vision of existence in such a complicated form it seems a labyrinth to the reader at first. So the writer must lead him along a private pathway of spatial and temporal patterns and personal relationships, until finally he awakens to the vision. Eventually the reader comes to realize that the paths themselves, like Christian's road to the Celestial City, embody much of the author's grand view of life.

Dickens's responses to the three parts of the serial challenge were brilliant assertions of his organic and unified vision of life over the technical difficulties. He solved the problem of spatial arrangement by creating a symbolic story world which overlapped installments and was always easily recognizable in individual incidents. However varied his incidents in any group of chapters, the reader could always grasp some relationship to the world of the whole book. He solved the problem of the constant need for advance in plot by creating a mystery plot which had alternating sub-lines. These swung back and forth between symbolically polar settings until a protagonist found eventual enlightenment and salvation. Thus Dickens could pursue any one of a number of characters' lives but still move forward in a general way. Finally, Dickens solved the problem of disconnected and undeveloped parts by concentrating more and more on the events in the life of a single passive protagonist who matured slowly and was freed from a more or less static situation of peril. Thus bits and pieces of plot became the parts and experiences of a developing personality.

These responses are interesting simply from the light they cast on Dickens or on individual novels he wrote. Yet it is more important that they are unusually vivid and complex examples of the characteristic solutions which novelists of many eras have used for the problems peculiar to the novel which I mentioned above. I refer, respectively, to metaphorical unity, polarity of plot and situation, and psychological continuity. These are the devices which permit the assertion of the novelists' organic and unified visions of life over the technical details and problems of this specific and peculiar form of storytelling. Yet they are not mere devices. They are some of the most important symbols in the *language* of the novel. A careful description of them can go far to define what the novel is. Such a definition can help us to get beyond the common notion that the novel is merely a single basic plot line with a moral which just happens to take 500 pages. Such a definition can help us also to see more in the novel than the mere elaboration of a basic metaphor which just happens to be in prose and to involve changes in time and place.

I believe, then, that I can explain part of the nature of the novel and part of the greatness of Dickens in a new and original way. The explanation and evidence I am going to present involve a good deal of new raw material and the details include a number of discoveries about Dickens.

PECULIARITIES
OF THE NOVEL

THE DETAILS of even a great artist's technique are
likely to seem overcomplex, confusing, and pointless if
approached abruptly and in isolation. Dickens is no
exception in this respect. It is the context of his artistic
decisions which shows the meaning and the deftness
of his technique. So we shall examine some of the
problems of the novel in general and proceed to Dickens's particular experiences of them in relation to the
serial. Then as we see how Dickens solved the problems, we will develop a sense of why he became a
novelist's novelist.

A reader is sometimes naturally led to ask himself the question, "What is a novel?" The same question occurs more insistently to the student and the
critic, and most of all to the novelist himself. J. Hillis
Miller thinks that Dickens in writing a novel was virtually creating himself and his identity. Mark Schorer
feels that a novelist, in writing, makes a discovery.

Other answers might be self-expression, prophetic revelation, voicing a people's dream, teaching, or construction of an esthetic stimulus, an escape, or an entertainment. Whatever one feels is going on in a general way, one is led to ask further, "Yes, but why this way and not in a short poem or a sculpture? What is a novel?" If we can describe a symphony or a Greek temple, and to a large extent with even geometric and mathematical precision—why not a novel?

Yet when we ask what a novel is (as opposed to what an "experimental" novel is or what a "novel of ideas" is), we find that we have few answers and that most discussion is vague and unsatisfactory.

The oldest definition of the novel pictured it as a story about realistic, everyday matters, and opposed to the romance, a story which dealt with the faraway in place and time, the exotic, and even the supernatural. Congreve, Fielding, Horace Walpole, Clara Reeve, Scott, Hawthorne, James all refer to this definition. Recently it has been put into Jungian psychological terms by Northrop Frye in his *Anatomy of Criticism.* Yet in many novels and consciously in the work of Scott, Trollope, George Eliot, and James, among others, "romance" and "novel" are combined; so this definition has proved unsatisfactory.

Later definitions are only a little more helpful. Friedrich Schlegel saw the novel as a literary genre including all the others—as the romantic, ironic product of an imagination operating freely. Such a view may help us appreciate aspects of *Finnegan's Wake,* but it does nothing for Trollope or Zola. Henry James saw the novel as a unified structure created by careful selection and skillful use of many tools. This idea is a sensible one, but James gave his readers a definition most of which might apply to many nonliterary works of art. The whole history of theoretical discussion of the novel and related art has been marked by a similar vagueness or a tendency to drift toward other issues. Critics like Burke and Hazlitt have tended to theorize about the effect of a book upon its audience. Others have been interested like Zola in a pictorial capturing of a reality outside of books or like Jeremy Collier in a moral organizing of that reality. Or like Friedrich Schlegel they have seen a book as the expression of its author's psyche. Some few have focused upon the work itself. They have studied its mechanical principles, as if it were music, as the Russian formalists like Toma-shevsky have done. Or they have studied the individual novel's organic form and relationships, as some New Critics have done. Yet only a very few like James have combined these four basic approaches even briefly and shed light on both the genre and individual works. In Appendix 4 I shall describe briefly the chief works with theories about story or theories importantly ap-plicable to story, especially the novel. The items come from classical, continental European, oriental, Eng-lish, and American literature, but almost all are disap-pointing. The ideas about story and about the novel in particular compose in virtually every case an external description or a general metaphor, not an operative analysis.

The average reader has not been troubled by this state of affairs, and it is a common idea that all kinds of stories are really much the same. Many a man will pass without any feeling of difficulty from discussion of an epic to discussion of a novel, or from discussion of a short story to discussion of a play. In part this is the influence of Aristotle, who placed so much empha-sis upon plot that he equated plot outline and story, as in his comments on the *Odyssey*. By this means he was able in most respects to equate tragedy and epic. There is some truth in this view, of course. We can see that a mistake causing misfortune, an heroic achievement, a union of two lovers, or a large number of other events can be presented in a drama, a ballad, a novel, a long narrative poem, or other forms, and we have a tendency to feel that the differences between the genres of story are obvious matters of acting out or singing, dramatic conversation or narration, and the like.

Yet when the avid novel reader turns to the *Iliad* or watches *As You Like It,* he finds they are sufficiently different from the novel to raise questions about this ancient idea: everything seems more out of focus than it would be in a novel; it is hard to discover what side everybody is on; and there is a curious lack of interest in the inner feelings of the characters. So this view is vague and unconvincing, too.

E. M. Forster, Ian Watt, and Wayne Booth point toward a more instructive approach. E. M. Forster in *Aspects of the Novel* attacked the emphasis on plot in the novel and, following the French critic Alain, suggested that the novel's great advantage was that it could present the private life of an individual. E. M. Forster, however, was completely captured by Bergson's idea that life is a disorderly but unified stream very different from the neat, dead boxes and forms into which reason and science cram it. So like Friedrich Schlegel he went to a view of the novel as virtually formless and lyrical. He insisted that the novel could be practically anything and denied that a really profound definition of it was possible.

Ian Watt in his *Rise of the Novel* has suggested that modern English society is individualistic and that the novel is a direct picture and expression of that society. Schiller and Friedrich Schlegel had believed rather similar things. To this individualism Watt relates the novel's realism and a number of its usual subjects. Watt, however, excludes the picaresque and, except by implication, does not go much beyond the idea of a direct picture and expression.

Wayne Booth in his *Rhetoric of Fiction* has just recently presented the view that a fiction is a complex rhetoric consisting of plot and other elements selected and arranged to persuade the reader to accept the world-view of the author. Essentially this seems an application of Aristotle's *Rhetoric* to the art of the novel and an extension of James's approach. Mr. Booth's particular interest lies in the analysis, within the context of this idea, of the use of points of view in the novel. Yet there is no reason why the idea of a rhetoric cannot be applied more broadly, as Mr. Booth seems to apply it in his first chapters.

Specifically I believe the best ideas of E. M. Forster, Watt, and Booth should be combined and extended. As I see it, the novel is a complex story rhetoric designed to present an individual's view of the world persuasively. Such a concept pictures the author as combining in a unified creation his interests in himself, the world in which he and his audience live, his audience, and his work itself. Moreover, I think the devices of the novel's rhetoric can be described and related to its nature and purpose.

Specifically I suggest that the novel's realistic detail, which Watt sees as a peculiarity of the genre and caused by its individualism, is a key never before used. It unlocks a whole complex of logically related features which are peculiar to the special type of story called a novel and are employed in it to define the world of the individual. Masses of detail require organization. So the novel requires a degree and kind of shaping not necessary to other types of story. The chief devices suggesting such shape in the novel are three: the novel uses *metaphor* to give an emotional overall organization to the detail; it uses *polarity* to give a personal feeling of the contrasts in the details and hence a feeling of change; it uses *psychological continuity* to give a sense of the working connection of various personal reactions to external details.

In this chapter I shall attempt merely to demonstrate briefly how detail, overall metaphor, polarity, and psychological continuity occur in the novel to a degree and with a frequency not found in the epic, the drama, the romance, etc. These, I believe, are some of the main peculiarities of the novel. None is merely a matter of plot, but each is a matter of structure and strategy. In later chapters I shall discuss the workings of each and show how the problems and solutions of Dickens let us examine these basic elements of the novel as if under a magnifying glass.

The use of much familiar detail from everyday life and everyday feelings has been said to be a feature of the novel, but it is worth indicating how very peculiar to the novel this feature is. Such detail, though often in a displaced setting, has been part of the novel's special charm from the first. What one remembers of *Don Quixote* is almost always the detail of real Renaissance Spain with which the wild but heroic don collides: windmills, a flock of sheep, a hogshead of wine, a barber's basin, a convoy of galley slaves, avaricious innkeepers, etc., etc. With *Robinson Crusoe* the detail had the same popularity. The simple descriptions of plants and animals, the accounts of making clothes and shelter (using what Defoe had observed of artisans in England) were imitated for more than a century to the endless delight of generations of readers—right down to that encyclopedic travesty, *The Swiss Family Robinson*. Dr. Johnson, furthermore, indicated that it is not plot or overall shape but details of sentiment which are the beauty of the novels of Richardson. We follow particular conflicts of feelings in Pamela or

Clarissa on particular occasions, or the books are meaningless. Readers of every generation have felt that one of the great attractions of Fielding is his vividly detailed pictures of life in the countryside and on the road in eighteenth-century England. In a similar way, details, whether external or internal, of nautical life, of landscape, of medieval life, of middle-class customs and dwellings have been responsible for much of the popularity of Smollett, Mrs. Radcliffe, Scott, and Dickens respectively. Of course the effects of hundreds of novelists like Cooper, Twain, Balzac, Zola, Tolstoy, Joyce have been similarly based in part on details from the private lives of individuals.

Nobody struggled so unsuccessfully to explain this feature of the novel as Fielding, who nobly attempted to describe his ideal of the new kind of storytelling. The Preface to *Joseph Andrews* and the first chapters of the books in *Tom Jones* reveal that Fielding labored mightily with the idea that the novel could be anything and with the idea that all kinds of story were more or less the same. He says that he is writing comedy, epic, prose, history, biography, etc. Yet at times he reverses himself, and perhaps he wrestles longest (at least in the prefaces and first chapters) with the idea that he is writing some kind of history. Essentially he tries to tell us that he is writing a made-up story which is realistic and detailed in a selective way. The organization of *Tom Jones*, his phrase the "comic epic in prose," his mechanical paralleling in *Amelia* of the incidents in the *Aeneid* indicate something else, however. This is the fact that he could not for long desert his attempt to model a novel on the epic or his Aristotelian belief in plot as the chief key to story. It is of course one important key. This continuing attempt may have been the source of his difficulties with definition, for in many ways the best method of seeing how

kinds of stories differ one from another is to compare
the epic and the novel. This is especially true if we
want to see how peculiar to the novel masses of familiar detail are. (A comparison of the novel and Greek
tragedy also suggests fundamental differences. In
another study, *Drama Before Aristotle,* I hope to show
how tragedy and the novel are boasts for society and
the individual respectively; how tragedy is deeply historical, the novel fundamentally wishful; how plot
serves different functions in the two genres; and
various other differences. It is enough to say here that
as soon as we stop concentrating on plot, careful comparison of the kinds of story reveals significant differences at once.)

If we examine the world's most finished epics, the
Iliad and the *Odyssey,* and compare them to various
typical English novels we find great differences in the
matter of detail. The *Iliad* and the *Odyssey* are very
long. We are told at length about the shield of Achilles
and the island of Circe and hundreds of other things:
the epic has detail. But it is neither everyday nor realistic detail. It is basically romantic and exotic. It is not
like the detail in Defoe's *Robinson Crusoe,* detail from
familiar life used in a faraway but accurately portrayed
setting. It is instead essentially foreign and sometimes
dwelt upon lovingly for this reason. The very fact that
in the *Iliad* there are details of fighting and weaponry
from half a dozen different stages of man's development—from the stone age to the age of iron—indicates
no consistent, thoroughgoing use of the detail of any
one period. Of course fighting is only one example of
the confusion of details of various ways of life in these
epics. The specific but never satisfactorily located
geography of the *Odyssey* is another. Furthermore,
obviously, such detail cannot be the furniture of some
one way of life faraway in place and time, as the detail

of an historical novel is. What is more, it is generalized and idealized and often formally paraded like the descriptions of dress or the catalog of ships. It is traditional and it is meant to suggest that there are specifics in the story world and that it is therefore momentarily to be believed, not to give clues in any but general, symbolic ways to the condition or feelings of the protagonist or other characters. The Greeks found minute and lengthy explorations of the individual's experience or feelings less interesting than the social and universal significance of his public acts. Accounts of the daily lives of characters are largely avoided— though their general nature is often briefly indicated as when Telemachus entertains Athene or Patroclus talks to Achilles in his tent or the gods hold council. The result is that the *Iliad* tends to drift away from being about some specific campaign and some specific warrior taking part in it and to become a poem about man in society within the encompassing battle of life itself. The *Odyssey* similarly drifts into an allegorical fantasy about the usefulness of man at home and the futility of man away. Both have great power and subtlety, and both are romantically sugarcoated, but neither is like a novel about Mycenaean Greece.

The novel is very different. *Clarissa, Robinson Crusoe, Joseph Andrews, Vanity Fair, Tess of the D'Urbervilles*, practically every novel you could name, is crammed with millions of details. We read about the characters' letters, their loves, their work, their worries, their hopes, the places where they eat, the gestures they make, the weather, etc.—about everything from the everyday life of the characters. Very often many of the details are familiar to the readers and are a part of their daily life also. Such a procedure lets every reader be judge of the reality of what he reads and to some extent lets him add the experience of the characters to his own. It also enables the author to suggest the specific psychological states of his characters. It makes possible elaborate pictures of the many activities of a character or a group and thus achieves semiacademic analyses of specific people or societies. The whole movement of the genre is closer to that of modern science than is the epic. Of course, the reader's reaction is often primarily esthetic, but the esthetic reaction can be likened more to a reaction to a representational painting than to an abstract, a form which the epic approaches.

In the matter of detail the novel is different not only from the epic but also from other kinds of story. Medieval romances like *Parzival, Lancelot,* the *Morte d'Arthur,* for example, have specific details, and their tournaments and castles and forest wanderings are presented at greater length than are the scenes in the Greek epics. Furthermore, these actions and settings are realistic as discontinuous bits and pieces and partly familiar as well. They are like tournaments, castles, and forest journeys experienced by their audiences. Yet the limitations of their realism are important. The combats, dress, and other externals are real enough, but much of Medieval external reality, especially its ugly side, is left out, as surviving unromantic Medieval literature reveals. The psychological states related to these externals are omitted or presented as stylized daring, fear, admiration, pride, humility, etc. The imperfect familiarity is also significant, for tournaments and castles are mixed with supernatural creatures and magic. The final result is that the detail of a Medieval romance is idealized and generalized and exoticized like the detail of an epic and presents another synthetic never-never land, not a picture of the world of its audience or of some earlier age. I do not wish to deny that generalizing, idealizing, exoticizing, and synthesizing take place in the composition of a novel also, but in the novel these processes are certainly modified by others and do not come so close to forming the whole of the work or its effect.

What about detail in other forms? The short story may employ realistic and familiar details, but by definition it does not use masses of them. Its aim is to produce a single brief effect or to make one point or present one picture; so it never brings in the masses of detail in the novel.

Most drama is somewhat similarly precluded from employing masses of realistic and familiar details by its very nature. Some dramatic pieces like the plays of Marlowe and Shakespeare and the Book of Job do present the feelings of individuals in great detail, but they are unusual. By and large drama, like epic, is public in its orientation, and it is public speech and the publicly significant in speech upon which it concentrates—hence its tendency to measure the individual comically or tragically against the group and the group's view of life. Details of setting are rare in dialogue and not even common in scenery in the thousands of years of dramatic history. Moreover, details of actions, except within a very few scenes and kinds of scenes, are excluded, as comparison with almost any adventure novel or detective story or movie will demonstrate.

Furthermore, the very brevity of drama militates against detail even in publicly significant speech: *Oedipus the King, The Misanthrope, Saint Joan* are almost generalized sketches of a few conversations compared to the developed presentations of conversations at length in the novels of Dickens or Meredith or many another author. Certain plays of Ibsen like *Hedda Gabler* which tried to approach the novel in its use of realistic and familiar detail are recognized as examples of a very special and not particularly successful subtype of the drama.

The point remains that most novels use vast masses of familiar and realistic detail and most other forms of story do not, and this fact poses a problem. If the reader is to feel some shape and direction in the novel—this internal, private kind of story—he must be helped. The problem is made more intense by the fact that the novel is a long fiction made up by an individual. It is not a well-known history, not a traditional myth, not a familiar heroic tale, not a short story. If the reader is to follow the story, if he is to make sense of the detail, enjoy it, and be convinced by it insofar as it serves a rhetorical purpose, it must have clear organization. That organization must be so clear that even in 300 to 600 pages the reader will not get lost as he might get lost if he set out to read an encyclopedia or a dictionary. A hack writer is content to set up a few crude guideposts and to concentrate upon the sensational appeal of the parts of his work. But the original and sincere novelist seeks to create an organization which will express his vision of life yet be so forceful that the reader will get a unified impression and not the disjointed effect of a newspaper. The more originally and thoroughly the author of a novel organizes the world familiar to the reader, the more the details at the start seem confusing to that reader. Paradoxically, this very organization reveals itself, removes this confusion, and leads to a perception of the artistic unity.

The three other peculiarities of the novel which I have mentioned, pervasive metaphor, polarity, and psychological continuity, are all means of organization. A long fiction with masses of realistic detail but without these other three devices would be more like a saga than a novel. The Icelandic saga is a fiction written in imitation of earlier historical accounts. It has the objective, public tone and public and rather tragic orientation of a history. Yet it gives detailed pictures of individual actions and speeches even in some private situations. Individual thought is suggested mainly by actions. There are large numbers of characters followed in the longer ones, the interest often shifting, as from Gunnar to Njal in *Burnt Njal*. The general social conditions and the nature of Icelandic life of the periods presented in the sagas were familiar to the saga audience through the earlier histories. The public and rather tragic orientation and this audience familiarity with the background spared the saga writer most of the task of the novelist. So the saga writer could be clear without using pervasive metaphor, polarity, and psychological continuity, though at first glance he may seem to have had the problem which they help solve.

The novel, however, does use these three devices. Let us look at pervasive metaphor first. The fascination of the present generation of critics with organicist ideas derived from the German Romantics, especially the notion of an overall metaphor in a work of art, has led to a special kind of criticism. It devalues poems lacking this particular kind of unity (and hence devalues many long poems) and suggests that all stories have the kind of unifying metaphor which these critics can find so easily in *Crime and Punishment* or *The Bear*. In fact, students nowadays tend to think that all unity and organization of a story are symbolic and tend to regard any attempt to demonstrate exceptions as attempts to deny the artistic value or intelligence of the works involved. Examination of epics, romances, short stories, plays, and sagas, reveals, however, that historical fact does not support this equation of symbol and unity. Some people see all plots as fundamental metaphors, but not all plots operate as such. Others detect overall metaphors independent of the plots, but not all stories contain them either.

For example, the plot of *King Lear* involves an old king's rejecting his loyal daughter, giving away her share of his kingdom to her villainous sisters, being rejected by them, and dying after his loyal daughter has failed in the attempt to help him and the other two have destroyed themselves. We could certainly say that one aspect of parenthood was a subject of the play. So are several aspects of kingship, some of which are parallel to the aspect of parenthood. Parenthood, however, is not an expressly symbolic device by which the story about it as a subject is systematically unified. There are two fathers and two sets of children with parallel plots of misjudgment and rejection, but there is no exploration of any parental relationships, as for the purposes of metaphorical suggestion, aside from the very specialized matter of misjudgments and rejections. Then the nonparental matters of kingship, pride, frankness, empty forms, treason, adultery, and madness are introduced into the plots and dialogue as independent but connected things not presented within the metaphor of parenthood. In fact, when we go to the poetry, we find that there are several unifying metaphors, not one: nothing, fool, nature, beast are perhaps the most famous, and none of these is particularly parental. Kingship, giving, expecting, rejection, ingratitude—we can try any of the forms in the plot in the same way: none becomes the one all-embracing metaphor. In *King Lear* plot does not operate like the single unifying metaphor in some short lyric poems, nor is there any other single unifying metaphor. We can feel that the play is a unity because we recognize

the shape of the type of plot, because we can follow the
flow and rhythm of the emotions expressed, and because we find a thematic unity in the dialogue.

What a different creation is even such an early
novel as *Robinson Crusoe.* Here the whole story of
what Defoe called his spiritual autobiography is dominated by the metaphor of the island. Robinson Crusoe,
by nature given to wandering, erring, sinning, is ship-
wrecked. This is a divine punishment, but his life is
spared. By hard work and economic ambition, and
with the humble acceptance of the help of events he
attributes to Providence, he manages to create some
safety and comfort on the island. The island itself
represents the essentially lonely life of man's soul on
earth surrounded by the unknowns and terrors of birth
and death. As Robinson says himself, he changes his
attitude toward God and life. He is then enabled to
save the life and teach the soul of another, Friday, and
finally to take sides with the captain in a battle against
evil forces and to be saved. This last event also involves leaving the island with both its terrors and its
satisfactions. Here the plot is certainly used meta-
phorically, though as part of the more inclusive metaphor of the island—dominant metaphors are very frequently metaphorical settings. Not only does the plot
emanate from the island. So do the emotions and
thoughts of Robinson and the reader, for the details of
Robinson's activities and other events and of Robinson's thoughts are pictured in a relation to the island
and Robinson's plight on it. Every aspect of the island
is developed for metaphorical purpose, and the vision
of the island informs most of the sentences of the
novel. Yet no vision of parenthood permeates long
stretches of *King Lear,* partly because the point of view
often shifts away from parental characters. In the
novel psychological continuity and polarity are used in

harness with pervasive metaphor. I will not quarrel with the man who says that almost all device and almost all life and even more all story are symbolic in some sense. Still I insist that here there is a difference of degree at least which is so great as to amount to a difference in kind and which represents a difference in conscious choice of artistic weapons.

The road of life metaphor in *Pilgrim's Progress* is just as plain as the island in *Robinson Crusoe*. In *Pamela* we find the image of life as a marriage of the individual to society. In forming the connection with society the individual, it is suggested, must remain true to principles and resist social pressures and leaders in order to achieve the kind of union the individual desires. In *Humphry Clinker* we have the metaphor of the provincial hypochondriac who journeys out into England and Scotland and into experience and contact with other people. Here he discovers a place for his activity in the lives of others and regains his health. The list can go on and on as hundreds of recent symbolic readings of novels show. We have the monster created by Science in *Frankenstein*, the geography of Highland wildness and English law and reason in *Waverley*, the proud firm of *Dombey and Son*, the prison of society in *Little Dorrit*, the fair itself in *Vanity Fair*, the evolutionary pattern in *The Way of All Flesh*, the jungle in *Heart of Darkness*, etc. The historical explanation may be that the early novelists inherited the tradition of Christian allegory and that later ones came under the influence of organicism, which pictured the world as symbolic concentrics. The functional explanation is that novelists were forced to use metaphor to tie familiar but fictional detail together and to give it shape and that they used the traditions which helped them.

As for romances and sagas, they are for the most

part like *King Lear* in not having dominant metaphors.
In the exceptions where there is a dominant metaphor,
it is so powerful and is pushed so hard that it is fairly
easy to see. In a very short moral romance like *Gawaine
and the Green Knight,* there is a metaphorical force to
the plot of the dedicated soul tempted by the flesh.
Here the plot is the effective metaphor, and all other
symbols are related to it. *Aucassin and Nicolette,* however, as well as *Parzival,* the story of Beaumains, the
English *Tristram,* and most others have nothing like
the island in *Robinson Crusoe* or the plot of the temptation of Gawaine. In fact many have no great unity or
unifying device. One looks in vain in the Eyrbyggja
Saga, the saga of Njal, and the others, some of which
are very skillfully unified, for any repeated, developed,
or overall symbol. In *Burnt Njal,* law is the subject.
Every degree of law and order, and every aspect, is
pictured. Yet the subject is pictured directly, because
the audience was familiar with the era and its conditions and occupations. Hence it could follow the detail as in a textbook without the help of a simplifying
and suggestive comparison or metaphor.

In the drama, there are two patterns in regard to
overall metaphor. Some Renaissance dramas follow
an allegorical tradition clearly and employ a unifying
metaphor. Examples are rebellion in *Henry IV,* Part I;
the island in *The Tempest;* the idea of nothing in *Much
Ado About Nothing;* the feud in *Romeo and Juliet;*
murder in *Macbeth;* delay in *Hamlet;* conquest in
Tamburlaine; knowledge in *Doctor Faustus;* animality
in *Volpone.* Yet, as I see it, though dozens of lesser
symbols are used, there is no extensive, systematic,
overall, unifying symbol in *Merry Wives of Windsor,
All's Well That Ends Well, Friar Bacon and Friar Bungay, The Jew of Malta, The Silent Woman, The Duch-
ess of Malfi, The Maid's Tragedy, Philaster,* and many

others which I would nevertheless insist had unity of idea and unity of effect and (in most cases) excellence. Most English drama of the Restoration seems to me like this latter group. On the other hand, Greek and French drama seem to me predominantly like the former—they seem to use overall metaphors.

The epic is a similar case. There is a journey alone in the *Epic of Gilgamesh,* but it is only a part of the story and does not unify it. The *Ramayana* and *Mahabharata* are vast sprawling works, the products of many hands. Yet even the main plot of each lacks a dominant metaphor. Other epics, the *Iliad,* the *Odyssey,* the *Aeneid, Paradise Lost, Beowulf,* are so directed at presenting a single, instructive general picture that it is not surprising to find that the allegorical force is concentrated in one inclusive metaphor. The work seems focused upon the fighting man within his nation at war, the return of the hero, the establishing within a chaotic world of the order of Rome, etc.

The use of a single unifying metaphor with allegorical purpose is characteristic, then, of the novel. It is on the whole avoided in some kinds of story and is present off and on in still others. Outside the novel, it is noticeably more common in stories written in poetry, a medium in which of course the metaphor seems natural.

Polarity, like pervasive metaphor, is a matter of degree. As the ancient Greeks realized, almost all stories polarize around a single basic conflict, however abstract or varied, but there are great differences in the degree to which this polarity is organized and simplified in outlines for the audience, whatever the complexity in parts. In the *Iliad* and *Paradise Lost* and in romances like *The Knight's Tale,* it is often difficult to tell with whom one sympathizes. In the *Iliad* and the *Epic of Gilgamesh* and the sagas and in romances like *Jerusalem Delivered*, it is often difficult to tell who is on which side or even if there are sides. Some of the same difficulty occurs in the drama, as in *Prometheus Bound, Hippolytus, Alcestis, As You Like It, Troilus and Cressida, Julius Caesar.* Yet almost anybody can see at once that Odysseus or Hamlet is pitted against his entire world, that Roland and other sincere men are opposed by the faithless. In slightly different stories, furthermore, most readers come to see that there are extensive, abstract, and subtle conflicts operating throughout. For example, we sense the struggle of law against chaos in the saga of Njal, of loyalty against neglect, misfortune, oppression in the *Ramayana*, of divine order against subjective barbarity in *Agamemnon*, and so on.

I suggest that in the novel a simplified polarity, either personal or abstract, is usually set up to help organize the mass of detail for the reader. In *Pilgrim's Progress*, Christian sets out for the Celestial City (heaven and salvation). Every thing, every event, every person, either helps or hinders him in his journey. *Robinson Crusoe, Moll Flanders, Pamela, Roderick Random* involve the posing for one protagonist of similarly simple problems to which everything is related. In fact many novels begin in this way and become subtler within the pattern. *The Sorrows of Young Werther, David Copperfield, Great Expectations, Manon Lescaut, The Ordeal of Richard Feverel, Esther Waters, Sons and Lovers* illustrate the principle. Others set up one protagonist against his or her environment and relate a succession of problems and every detail to the broad struggle between protagonist and environment. *Don Quixote, The Vicar of Wakefield, Oliver Twist, Jane Eyre, The Mill on the Floss, The Red and*

the Black, Madame Bovary, Man's Fate, Young Lonigan
follow this pattern. This type may grow out of an
overlap with the previous one. Another type takes a
single great problem or situation and sets up a series
of people against it, as in *Ivanhoe, Hard Times, Little
Dorrit, Middlemarch, Vanity Fair, War and Peace,
Barchester Towers, Wuthering Heights, Nostromo, The
Sound and the Fury.* Still another sets up one protagonist with an internal problem against an environment with a problem or conflict or complex situation.
Humphry Clinker and *Crime and Punishment* and
Ulysses and *Heart of Darkness* and *Lord Jim* with their
troubled heroes in troubled societies involve this kind
of confrontation. Other variations and combinations
are possible, but the point is that in the novel the conflict is almost always pronounced and obvious.

In a novel with many important characters, most
are set up in parallels or clusters, and shifts in point
of view (as from Dorothea Brooke to Lydgate to Fred
Vincy in *Middlemarch* tend to involve shifting from
one battler to another on the same side or in a parallel
position. The shifts of point of view in the epic, however, often cross the battle line so we take opposing
points of view. Such shifts occur very frequently in
the *Iliad,* the *Ramayana, Paradise Lost.* We find the
same crossing in the sagas, and in dramas the tendency
is exaggerated by giving individuals on opposing sides
many lines of dialogue each. *Medea, Prometheus
Bound, The Trojan Women, Oedipus the King,* the
great tragedies of Marlowe and Shakespeare are brilliant exceptions to this dramatic pattern. The more
usual kind of thing is seen in *Hippolytus* or *The Country Wife.* Obviously this shifting of point of view
across battle lines accompanies a tendency to make less
of polarity. In the more socially oriented ancient world
which produced the epic and the drama, an intense

awareness of individual conflict and situation seemed less important that it does now.

    Psychological continuity is obviously related to polarity and point of view. It is perhaps the most obvious of the unifying patterns peculiar to the novel. It has often been admired in the novel since Goethe's *Sorrows of Young Werther*, but was important even earlier. Of course, the internal quality of the novel has been noted since Schiller and Friedrich Schlegel, but continuity is essential to this quality. Psychological continuity is missing from the epic. Our interest in the *Iliad* moves from Achilles to the Greek generals to the Trojans to the gods to the Greek troops to Achilles and off again, a dozen different times. It is not the story of Achilles, but, as Homer says, of the wrath of Achilles and its effects. In the *Odyssey* the situation is the same. We start by overhearing the council of the gods. Then we look at the conditions in Ithaca. We come to focus on Telemachus. We watch Odysseus leave the isle of Calypso, be wrecked upon the sea, and come to stay with the Phaeacians. We drop back and follow his adventures in a three-year period ending seven years before and told in the first person. We move forward, in a story told once more in the third person, to follow, in the last third of the book, his landing in Ithaca and the reactions of various people to him and his victory. Even in this last section, where at times we seem to be following an action of Odysseus steadily, the movement is broken up by several long conversations with the swineherd. In neither epic do we see into the minds and hearts of the protagonists for more than a scattered moment or two at a time—a procedure which comes as a surprise to the modern reader. In both epics we move suddenly from earth to heaven and back again after a scene or so. The reason is plain enough. The group-oriented Greeks were only reluctantly interested in the individual, though passionate enough in that partial interest. Essentially, in their epics as in their tragedies, they were telling public stories. What was important was how the action of Achilles fitted into a grand, cosmic-and-earthly social scheme. What was to be perceived was how Odysseus' adventuring and heroism produced social consequences disastrous at first but then ultimately curative, as he was pulled back into his home and country. The private feelings of Achilles and Odysseus seemed less important, though they are indicated in some speeches and actions.

It is easy to see the difference between such narratives and those to be found in *Robinson Crusoe, Pamela, Pride and Prejudice, Great Expectations, Ulysses,* etc. A continuous tracing of the adventures of a psyche is fundamental to the novel. The shifts in point of view in novels like *Tristram Shandy, Dombey and Son, Middlemarch, Lord Jim,* etc., are only superficial deviations from this psychological continuity. It does not matter that some novels trace the adventures of several psyches. It is important that this whole method, this continuous intimate procedure, is fundamentally different from the epic type of narration conducted from outside the hero. The shifting that permits Homer to give us pages and pages of a catalog of ships in the *Iliad* is not the shift from the inside of one psyche to the inside of another, but a shift from one portion of a vast canvas painted all at arms length to another portion of the same thing. The creator of the saga is often closer to the canvas, but his general procedure in this matter is like that of the epic poet.

When we look at the drama and the romance we find much the same discontinuity of psychology which we found in the epic. There are exceptions in *Oedipus the King* and in the great tragedies of Shakespeare, but the vast majority of Greek dramas like Aeschylus' *Agamemnon, Seven Against Thebes, The Persians, The Suppliants,* Sophocles' *Trachiniae, Oedipus at Colonus,* Euripides' *Bacchae, Trojan Women, Rhesus, Orestes, Children of Heracles, The Suppliants, Iphigenia in Aulis,* and most of the comedies of Aristophanes do not attempt psychological continuity, nor is it common in English drama of the Renaissance. *As You Like It, Much Ado About Nothing, The Tempest,* even *Henry IV,* Part I, *Julius Caesar,* and most of the lesser plays present us with conversations and incidents involving a bewildering multitude of people. The drama is essentially a social thing. Although a good play has unity and organization, it is not usually the unity and organization provided by psychological continuity.

In the romance we have a form of literature in which the switching from one incident to another and from one hero to another is famous. Certainly some simpler romances follow the fortunes of a single man episodically, but they do not follow his thoughts or emotions constantly. It is true we see a man riding on his horse, we see him fighting a dragon or another knight, or rescuing a lady, but we have no sense of the steady or jagged inner movement of his mind and heart as he goes through these adventures.

The case can be continued in shorter narratives before those of recent times. The Miller's Tale, the parable of the Prodigal Son, Boccaccio's story of the man who pretends to be dumb and is given a job at a convent, and many others exhibit the same external view of the individuals and the same jumping about of the narrative.

Whatever else it may involve, then, the novel is peculiar in its use of great masses of familiar and realistic detail and in its use of pervasive metaphor, polarity, and psychological continuity. We have observed the systematic and central position of these features in the novel and have seen that they are logically related to each other as a rhetorical complex and to the origin, purpose, and nature of the novel itself. In later chapters we shall see how each of these features becomes a contribution to the individualistic vision of life and gives shape to the mass of details in the novel, and we shall see how the serial posed the organizational problems of the novel in such oversimplified form that it actually helped Dickens attain greatness.

METAPHOR AND
THE PROBLEM OF
ARRANGEMENT IN THE NOVEL

FREQUENTLY these days a novel is considered a system
of symbols or the extension of a basic metaphor. Yet
the reader of novels finds this one mainly a story, that
one mainly a symbol, a third a direct description of a
mind or a society, etc. The novel may be a complex
thing with several parts, any one or any combination
of which may receive emphasis in a particular example.
But what is the nature of the total creation? Several
propositions may afford us a glimpse of one part or the
other. In developing such propositions we may over-
emphasize some one aspect. Moreover, it is at least as
interesting to attempt to keep our eyes upon the complexity itself. This much is clear: the difficulty in defining a novel is no accident. Every good novel makes
us ask ourselves: "What is it?" Amid the fantastic
variety, we do not know what to expect when we begin
to read.

There are various external attempts to help readers, but none of them works very well. Perhaps we hear from a friend that such and such a novel is good and is this or that particular kind of thing, but friends often see things very differently. I remember being told, "*Tristram Shandy* is wonderful. It is the story of Toby, a retired soldier. . . ." Sometimes we read the dust jacket of a book or a review, but as often as not the writer of such a thing sees a book from an angle even stranger than a friend's. In the long run, we find other people's reactions misleading often enough to bring us to each novel asking "What is it?"

Because it uses so many familiar details from everyday life, the novel, whatever the author's purpose, presents a picture of the world. A story is by its nature representational, of course, but one peculiarity of the novel is its intensification of this feature. To some extent the novel is, as Fielding said long ago, a tasty dish for our pleasure (even if a mysterious one). Since its contents are clearly human life, the good novel not only keeps us wondering "What is it?" but leads us to ask "What, then, is human life?" It begins, then, as a pleasing mystery, with far-reaching implications.

Calculated increasing of curiosity or suspense may keep a novel a mystery for a long while, but even without these things a novel is likely to remain a mystery for some time to its reader. It may do so even after he has finished the book, for a novel is not a short lyric poem, an expository statement, or an account of well-known history, but the highly individualized vision and creation of one man presented in enormous and difficult detail. So it does not declare or reveal itself quickly and frankly.

Faced with a question, we try to answer it. Faced with a mystery, we try to unravel it. The novelist, willy-nilly, helps us to the answers we find. As a result, he becomes involved in questions of the nature of reality, of the nature of learning and knowing, of the nature of the devices by which one leads others to learn and know. By whatever terms he calls his tools, he shapes an answer to the questions "What is this novel?" "How can the reader tell?" "Why did the author write it?" "What is life for this writer and perhaps for me?" The novelist's work becomes, to some extent, an orientation of the reader, an orientation which may satisfy or disappoint. In consequence, a large part of the technique of the novel is related to this matter.

It is not really strange that the novel involves an orientation, for the novelist has much more freedom to do and say what he pleases with his audience than other kinds of writers have had. He has also a much greater burden of building. The tragedian, the epic poet, the writer of romances had certain advantages over the novelist when they began composing. Their plots were usually tales of public events known to their audiences in many cases. The settings and the human conditions involved in their stories were also known. Often meter and language and general style were predetermined as well. By comparison the novelist begins with a piece of paper far more nearly blank. This blankness is the freedom of the sincere and original novelist to present the world as he sees it and to write in any manner about anyone in any circumstances. It is also a problem. The reader knows nothing about the world in the novelist's story or about the people, and the novelist must interest other persons in his work even to get his book published, let alone sold.

This ignorance of the reader about the people in a novel is in many ways more important than his ignorance of the novelist's world. If one man is to talk to another about an individual, then he has to fill in what may be completely unknown, for we know little about the private lives of other individuals unless they or their intimates tell us. Each of us is so ignorant about some other people that he asks himself commonly, "How can he stand that kind of work?" "What did she ever see in him?" and so on. This privacy and anonymity are part of the urban life of modern individualistic society.

Whatever the cause, the results for the novelist are clear. He must work hard to help his audience in ways the storytellers of earlier days did not need to trouble themselves about. The organization supplied to epic and tragedy by tradition or by the dance, the novelist must create synthetically and supply himself. Furthermore, he must take great care with his organization for it must control great masses of familiar details, dull or confusing by themselves but always composing much of the substance of his kind of writing. He is likely then to be conscious of, and deliberate about, his organization, and it is usually a very sturdy and prominent feature of his work. Ancient poet-prophets, in contrast, were spoken of frequently as mad, inspired, or wildly emotional, and many of their works seem disorderly.

Since it is detail about the private lives of one or more persons which requires organization in the novel for the individual reader, it is natural that the instruments of organization in the novel have some significant relation to individual life. The reader starts out in an unknown world of unknown characters. He cannot predict his own reactions to these characters, but he does have certain private methods of orienting himself in unfamiliar situations in real life, and the novelist strives to encourage him to use these as he reads. Thus the novel can be a sort of proving ground of our theories of perceiving, learning, and knowing. As the subsequent discussion will suggest, a number of prevalent theories, particularly those of Hume and Kant, do not seem altogether satisfactory under such testing. Two centuries ago Lessing in *Laocoon* was exploring the arts in relation to perception of space and time, and the method has been popular at various times since. Yet I must insist that there are still many discoveries to be made by using this method systematically.

In life, when faced with the unknown as he is frequently, the individual tries to find out where he is, what is happening, and how he interacts with the world. In other words, he seeks to establish a geography, to develop an awareness of shapes which are changing, and to develop a feeling of the nature of his continuous life. When he feels the same need as he reads a novel, the novelist encourages him to seek similar orientation by supplying him with a pervasive metaphor, a sharp polarity of situation, and a continuity of psychological states. Thus the reader, as he identifies himself with the protagonist of the novel—far more closely than with the protagonists of ancient works—is led to experience the mass of details in the novel as an (increasingly) organized unit.

The most fundamental of these problems and solutions is the desire to know where one is and where any given detail fits and the establishment of an all-inclusive geography. The pervasive metaphor is the answer attempted by the individual. It is equally natural to think in terms of one all-inclusive thing, the universe, or of untold billions of things, like atoms. Whatever may be the truth, man often tries to perceive everything at once. When we climb to the top of a mountain and look down the other side for the first time, we do not behave as some philosophers claim we do. We do not react to endless atoms of green and blue and brown and white, then slowly, employing our imagination, organize them into a unity. No—we perceive at once the magnificent sweep of the view.

Such perception is both a complex sensation and a direct recognition by the brain. The retina contains thousands of rods and cones which simultaneously react individually like the different areas on a film to variations of color, light, etc. These give us at one instant a sensation which registers details and relationships and shapes or the absence of these in the view. Since the retina is physiologically a portion of the brain, this sight, unlike other sensations we may have, becomes knowledge directly. The complexity and directness of seeing make us trust it much more than other senses. Apparently our vision of shapes and relationships depends on some cooperation of external patterns and internal ones involved in the still partly unknown nature of the eye.

It is only after all this that we fall to picking out individual lakes, rivers, trees, leaves, houses, and automobiles below. It is only later that we imagine the sights from other mountains and from far below. Man frequently attempts such Olympian perception in regard to life as a whole. Indeed much of religion, philosophy, learning, science, and story is an effort to produce it. The ancient Greek idea of the cosmos, or a reality like an orderly human town, and the Hebrew worship of Jehovah as creator of heaven, earth, man, and moral law are only two of the most widely known and formalized of these efforts. Like all other attempts to express an overall view, they involve metaphors: reality is like a town in which there are rules and collective efforts, or the human is like a pot shaped in obedience to the fingers of its creator and failing that reduced to pliant clay again. Metaphors are substitutes for and simplifications of things. Often all one can hope from them is to recognize the tune or to grasp the rhythm or to catch the spirit of the object compared, as when we find Spenser calling the lily "the lady of the garden." Sometimes, however, a great metaphor can be extensively pursued, as when the seventeenth- and eighteenth-century scientist saw the world as a machine whose workings observant men could discover and control. Overall metaphors are of this latter kind.

The novelist is to some extent in the position of presenting an unknown universe of which he is the priest, philosopher, poet, and scientist. The world of his novel is itself a substitute and oversimplification, but it is still so vast that it needs reduction to a metaphor, preferably one so clever in its new implications that it will justify the initial foreshortening of life itself. It must be a huge metaphor capable of extensive development because of the nature of the problem it is chosen to solve.

This metaphorical geography is essentially an emotional method of measurement or assessment. The place and value of most individual things within any one of these grand metaphorical schemes can be seen at a glance. Within the cosmos or universal city, the man who does not know the laws or breaks them is a fool and will be punished, and any voice raised for order or harmony is a good voice. In a world watched over by its creator, history is a pattern flowing from divine intention. In a mechanical world, steam takes up more space than water, so that if it can be harnessed, it will turn wheels, and the foxes keep down the rabbits, so that if the foxes are exterminated, vegetable gardens get overrun. All assessment is comparison, but the sweep of these great metaphors encourages quick and impulsive assessment. The philosophers and scientists may not use such metaphors for emotionally evaluative purposes, but rather for their usefulness in exploration or teaching. Yet this fact cannot obscure the tendency of such metaphors to become like ancient myths accepted as absolute truths in the minds of the general public and then used as quick standards of ultimate evaluation. With such evaluation comes the emotional load.

The poet and storyteller make use of this human tendency and employ metaphors that will guide their audiences to a quick and passionate grasp of the essence of what they have to say. As a matter of fact, Alfred Harbage in *As They Liked It* associates all the emotional power of Shakespeare's poetry with his constant use of ideas of evaluation in metaphors. Again and again Shakespeare measures the value of a thing or an act against what is right or what is natural or what is reasonable, implying or stating the truth of some broad or universal metaphor. Yet he does not systematically base each of his stories on one vast metaphor.

The novelist does. In his hands every hint of relationship to a broad central metaphor becomes an emotional signpost indicating the whole geography of the novel and the value of any given detail. The technique which uses such a device becomes a pathway through the labyrinth of the novel.

The Victorian novelist with what was frequently his or her 800-page work had a particular need for the pervasive metaphor. George Eliot's *Middlemarch* is a good example. This novel has eight or more important characters; perhaps fifty minor ones. Many of the affairs of a town during the period of about a decade are presented, and dozens of private events are included. The reader needs help and gets it. We pass from the title with its suggestion of provincial life to the idea of St. Theresa, a nun and hence *married* to God, and to the satisfaction of her need for action by the reforming of a religious order. From this thought we pass to the idea of the need of woman in general to satisfy herself, then to Dorothea. The name links

God and love again. She is compared to Don Quixote
and is shown trying to satisfy her obvious need to be
busy and to do good by helping some local cottagers.
For a while Dorothea thinks of *marriage* to a half-
sympathetic but stupid squire as a way to carry out her
plans. Then we follow Dorothea as she tries *marrying*
the elderly clergyman Casaubon and helping him with
what turns out not to be a great work. Then we pass
to Lydgate, a young doctor new to the town of Middlemarch and eager to modernize its medicine and found
a hospital there. We see him become naïvely entangled
in the petty politics connected with the establishment
of the hospital and are told that men have to adjust to
the pressures and accept the web of relationships in
society. We follow him as he falls in love with Rosamund Vincy and the wealthy life, then as he *marries*
Rosamund and finds her and the life of status unsatis-
fying and degrading. We are told men's subjective
dreams do not match realities. We are told that a
career is like a *marriage,* and then we are shown the
love and the struggle toward a career of Fred Vincy—
ending finally, we can foresee, in a happy *marriage*
and career. Dorothea's husband dies, and she becomes
the helper and savior of the rather aimless esthete Will
Ladislaw. Eventually she keeps Rosamund's *marriage*
from collapsing altogether and *marries* Ladislaw, now
a reform politician.

The whole story is developed around the image
of life as a marriage, which Eliot got from Feuerbach.
Marriage is shown mostly as a beginning not an end—
as the basic confrontation of the subjective, romantic,
single individual full of illusions with hard and social
reality in which the individual is but a part of a com-
munal progress. We are not hit over the head with the
image of marriage, but, even if we miss the implica-

tions of the St. Theresa-Dorothea parallel and of many hints along the way, we note the blending in Dorothea of the urge to work and the urge to marry and we see in Lydgate the parallel to Dorothea. The general organizing principle is thus gradually impressed upon us even before the direct statements about the basic symbol, which occur sooner or later in most novels, however briefly.

Even in the early pages such details as the unconsciousness and triviality of Dorothea's sister have a clear relation to our feeling at that point for the whole world of the book. We perceive that the sister will lead a perfectly happy life as long as she is protected by the work and wealth of others. She is superficially aware of social reality. Obviously the great mistakes and great achievements which are dimly felt possibilities for Dorothea will not be her lot. Emotionally the symbolic organization guides us here also. We find the sister charming. We sympathize profoundly with Dorothea, are exhilarated by her ambitious nature, but fear for her happiness. And so it goes throughout the book. Lydgate arouses in us some of the same feelings that we have for Dorothea, but we are first disappointed and then repelled by his weak departures from principle and his captivation by surfaces. We pity his failure to come to satisfactory terms with his career or his wife. The other characters and all the detail of their lives, although this is an unusually discursive and undramatic novel, are similarly given a color and value for us by the central metaphor of marriage. Thus George Eliot organizes all of the material, from Casaubon, the would-be cannibal, to the loyal Mrs. Bulstrode; from the study of mythology bogged down in ego-asserting quarrels to Lydgate's ruinously expensive furniture. Everything is measured by the metaphor of marriage and the love, cooperation, work, responsibility, adjustment, maturing, productivity, progress, experience, etc. that we associate with marriage.

The mechanical problem of masses of familiar detail was greatly exaggerated for Dickens, and the organic solution by means of a pervasive metaphor was the more brilliantly and dynamically employed by him. First, he was the earliest novelist to write mainly about the common middle-class people of England in their customary surroundings. So the familiarity of detail was even more of a problem to him. While it was a great pleasure to his audience, it did accentuate his difficulties. Exotic detail is easy to remember; the familiar we are likely to confuse with our own lives or overlook or despise. Second, and more important here, serialization in effect magnified the size of the novel and the degree to which its meaning, context, organization (if not its detail) were unknown to the reader.

Edward Chapman and William Hall visited Charles Dickens in 1836 and proposed that he write some serial adventures of a club of sportsmen to accompany sets of humorous sketches. Dickens insisted that the text must have an existence of its own. Chapman and Hall agreed. And Dickens, despite his friends' warnings, began the serial writing and publication which he continued through all his fifteen novels and thirty-four years. While five novels appeared first as weekly serials in periodicals of which Dickens was editor, the others appeared first in monthly portions like *Pickwick Papers*. Most of the books were very long, as were many other Victorian novels. Virtually all were absorbed by their readers over an unusually long period of time: a year to over a year and a half. In the first three and in most later cases, the reader was presented with an installment of three or four chapters, then left to wait for a month, then presented with three or four more chapters, then left to wait for another month, and so on. If a long novel with masses of familiar detail presents the reader with a mystery so confusing he requires help, a long novel with masses of familiar detail delivered in batches with month-long gaps between them over a period of nineteen months might have been expected to present an almost insuperable obstacle. The problem of the reader's needing to know where he was and where this or that detail fitted was very pressing. It was pressing not only at the beginning of the novel but again and again at points during the novel when new installments began and the reader might have forgotten or confused this or that pattern during the month-long intervals before. The same problem was not only present throughout the novel, but was intensified to a point of mental emergency because the reader held in his hands only a tiny fraction of the novel at a time.

Dickens, like all serial writers, was tempted to use various cheap devices to solve this problem. Unlike many other serial writers, Dickens was impelled to present a profound vision of life and worked during his career to order the serial and make it the vehicle of his vision. We shall see in the next chapter that he wrote his serial novels while they were being published, that he used stock characters and multiple plots. Yet he worked hard and took great pains with characterization, and in the chapter after next we shall see that he created symbolic worlds in which his character types fit and were justified and from which proceeded great parallels and contrasts which tied together his many plots.

Every novel to some extent is composed of individual chapters, scenes, sequences, movements, or whatever, with pauses between them. Moreover, many passages in any novel, descriptions, bits of dialogue and characterization, even some actions, could be put in any one of several movements. The longer and the more complicated the novel, the more there is some freedom and some problem in such arrangement. This arrangement is really the matter of where the reader is and where a given detail fits at a microscopic level. If an author neglects it, he is leaving the reader adrift for short periods of time. We shall see in the next chapter that serial publication encouraged Dickens, like most serial writers, to pack his installments with lots of incidents, selected for variety, and to arrange these slightly to give each installment a pattern of its own independent from the rest of the novel. Yet in the chapter after that we shall see that this serial tendency also was tamed, for Dickens's symbolic visions overflowed individual installments and pulled together and gave pattern to the most disparate of materials. This symbolic unification became more and more important to Dickens, but was always one of his triumphs. It is as if, presented with a medium which fell naturally to pieces, he learned to picture every detail and every event in symbolic relationships so that his novels seem dazzling in their many-sided evocativeness and connection, their magnificent flow of meaning.

SOME
TEMPTATIONS OF
SERIAL COMPOSITION

DICKENS'S METHODS of serial composition placed a huge obstacle in his way at the very start by encouraging him to deal with story materials with the coolness of a grocer setting up a display of vegetables. He wrote with less planning than most novelists employ. He deliberately packed his installments with exciting incidents. He used stock characters and incidents, though with great skill and energy. He made his serial installments artistic units with specific patterns, and he considered a serial story one which could be easily divided.

As the 1847 Preface of *Pickwick Papers* tells us, Dickens rediscovered the serial form accidentally,[1] and the huge success of this first novel led him to continue writing in somewhat the same form. His whole procedure would have prevented a lesser man from writing novels at all. Dickens wrote his novels as he published them, in monthly or weekly installments.[2] He rarely completed a monthly number much more than ten days before it was to be printed and considered being four weeks ahead of the printer his customary advance in the weekly serials.[3] He saw none of his novels as a completed whole until after the last installment was written. Hence he could not revise.[4] Yet he probably would not have revised if he could have, for he mentions in a letter to Bulwer-Lytton an "insuperable aversion" to reworking an idea.[5]

Not only did he write as he was printed; he did much of his planning that way and did incredibly little planning, at that. Forster says, "Before beginning any number of a serial, he used . . . to plan what he intended to put into it chapter by chapter."[6] His notes and plans for many of his novels have survived and have been analyzed in detail by John Butt and Kathleen Tillotson.[7] Mr. Fielding shrewdly sums up the nature of these papers when he says that they consisted "partly of suggestions of what was to be done and partly of a rough outline of the story as far as he had gone."[8] In general the notes are largely lists, usually of concrete subjects: people, events, names, places. By and large they are concerned with the naming and placing in order of characters and events and things to be described or narrated. They do not dig as deeply into the meanings and intentions and problems of a whole book or of his writing in general as bits of Dickens's letters sometimes do. Even the letters show that much of Dickens's planning and thought were concerned with the effect of individual installments. There are several letters to Forster about *Dombey and Son*, for example; all but the first one or two emphasize individual installments.[9] During the composition of *Barnaby Rudge*, Dickens wrote to Forster, " 'the contents of one number usually require a day's thought at the very least.' "[10]

Only one outline of a whole novel in Dickens's

words has come down to us, though some others may
have existed. This is the rough general description of
Dombey and Son given to Forster in a letter.[11] Forster,
however, describes the general plan of *Edwin Drood* as
communicated to him by Dickens "before any of the
book was written."[12] Probably some such vague overall shape existed in most cases. Many letters appear to
indicate this fact, the one describing the origin of
Great Expectations or Forster's discussion of *The
Chimes* (see below), for example.

    The external evidence, then, indicates that Dick-
ens's method of composition involved devoting considerable time and energy to a kind of arranging of
things, mostly characters and incidents. For this arranging process these things were conceived of as
rather static qualities.

    An examination of the novels chapter by chapter,
installment by installment, shows the results of this
method (see Appendix 1 for a description of all the installments in every Dickens novel). Every installment
near the start of a novel is full of new characters, and
every installment is carefully packed with incidents.
There are half a dozen or more incidents in the regular
installments of those serials which appeared as
monthly paperbacks. Only one or two incidents, however, make up the lean installments of the novels
which were serialized in periodicals (*Oliver Twist, The
Old Curiosity Shop, Barnaby Rudge, Hard Times, A
Tale of Two Cities,* and *Great Expectations*). Most installments have at least one sensational incident, at
least one (perhaps the same incident) which is a surprise, and one event which arouses curiosity or anxiety
or both. Often every installment contains a great variety of event and mood. This packing is so obvious
that two brief illustrations will do. The third installment of Pickwick contains the card party, the Con-

vict's Return, the shooting of Tupman by Winkle, the cricket match, Tupman's kissing Miss Wardle, Jingle's overhearing the fat boy, Jingle's tricking Miss Wardle, Jingle's tricking Tupman. Three typical installments of *Barnaby Rudge* can be summarized thus: In installment sixteen Chester deceives Emma Haredale about his son, and Joe Willet rebels against his father and pummels one of his father's friends. In installment seventeen, Joe runs away and meets a recruiting sergeant; he says goodbye to Dolly Varden, who is indifferent, and enlists; Edward and his father (Chester) part for good. In installment eighteen, Daisy sees a ghost, and old Willet goes out through a storm and tells Mr. Haredale.

This packing requires Dickens to tell stories about several different people and subjects in one novel in order to include enough incidents. *Dombey and Son* is typical. On a simple external level, it is a mixture of several stories, Florence's, Walter's, Paul's, Dombey's, Edith's. The fact that Dickens usually looks over the shoulder of first one character and then another emphasizes this fact. Thus in the thirty-one chapters of the first half of the novel, if we allow half for each where a chapter is about two people, we find a chapter-by-chapter outline of the novel shows that there are seven chapters about Paul, six about Walter, five and a half about Florence, four and a half about Dombey. Thus Dombey gets only about a sixth of the space, despite the fact that the general plan of the book makes Dombey clearly the main character. In addition, there are, in this half, two chapters about Carker, two about Bagstock, one and a half about Edith, and one each about Cuttle and Miss Tox. Taken as a whole, the book combines two Cinderella stories (Florence's and Walter's), a reform story (Dombey's), a parallel to Little

Nell's decline (Paul's), a sympathetic near-adultery (Edith's).

Martin Chuzzlewit, when examined chapter by chapter, proves to be a mixture of at least three stories, young Martin's reform, Pecksniff's hypocrisy and exposure, Jonas Chuzzlewit's murder and capture. *David Copperfield* combines David's boyhood terrors, the Steerforth-Emily plot, the Dora-Agnes-David love affair. The other novels are similar.

The process of arranging characters and incidents as if they were so many static quantities also led, fantastic as the variety of the finished product may make it seem, to the use of stock characters and incidents. Dickens's characters are of certain kinds only. Virtually all his hundreds of characters are from one or more of the following groups: avaricious lawyers, wicked businessmen, avaricious criminals, people avaricious in private life, mysterious enemies, malicious wrongdoers, fanatical "Christians," other fanatics, haughty or useless aristocrats, shrewish wives, unpleasantly aggressive females, "betrayed" women, people cut off from the world, hard, proud people, selfish, proud people, women oppressed by male relatives, women oppressed by husbands or lovers, prisoners, impoverished people, thoughtless young men, people incapable of handling money, failures, childlike characters, people disfigured or injured in mind or body, wards or orphans, sympathetic children, sympathetic older men, saintly young women, guardians, kind old gentlemen, eccentric, kindly clerks, unsuccessful lovers, faithful servants. It is a long list but clearly does not include all human types. A table illustrating this list in detail will be found in Appendix 2. A justification for calling these characters (and his incidents) "stock" is the fact that contemporary and later melodrama (see M. Wilson Disher, *Melodrama*, New York, 1954, p. xiv) and eighteenth-century novels of sensibility and terror are full of similar elements. Appendix 2 will also show evidence, however, that Dickens thought in these categories to some extent.

Their eccentricities make the various representatives of the basic types appear so different from one another that their typical quality is hidden. Thus Newman Noggs in *Nicholas Nickleby*, Pancks in *Little Dorrit*, and Wemmick in *Great Expectations* are all basically clerks and all basically odd, but they appear to be different. Noggs is an ex-gentleman, with queer eyes. He drinks. His suppressed dislike of his employer shows up in extraordinary grimaces. Pancks is described more than once as going around like a steam engine. He is very businesslike. His hobby is missing heirs. Wemmick is two men, one at work, the other at home. He supports an old father in a quaintly landscaped home. He has a girl friend whom he marries in the least conspicuous way possible. These three clerks all appear to be different personalities, indeed are almost different people, but they all perform the same action, as do the six other clerks listed with them in Appendix 2. They help other characters from their special position as men intimate with business.

Let us look at another group, "wicked businessmen." Bounderby, the boastful self-made man in *Hard Times*, Heep, the hypocritical snake in *David Copperfield*, and Smallweed, the loan shark in *Bleak House*, all do the same things. They get money for themselves at the expense of other people by exploitation, embezzlement, and extortion respectively. The same thing is true of the other groups of characters. There are a *few* exceptions but 95 per cent or so of each group behaves in one way.

Suppose we try substituting Wemmick for Noggs,

Bounderby for Smallweed. Can the stories go on as before? Certainly. We can do the same with the members of other groups in any book of Dickens's. We may have trouble with half the members of one group. Dombey, Gradgrind, Dorrit, Mrs. Defarge, Miss Havisham, Magwitch in the group called "fanatics in private life" are so strongly twisted in their peculiar ways, and those ways are so much a part of the protagonists' situations, that they could not be interchanged. But practically all the other members of all the groups can be exchanged for other members of the same sex and same group. This interchangeableness shows us that the differences in character, if any, between members of any one group are almost always ones which are not important to the plot.

The incidents used by Dickens fall into similar categories. (Some of the situations and incidents have been included in my classifications of character.) Oppression, murder, rejection, inheritance, imprisonment, marriage, flight, death, obsession, madness, mob violence, illusions, rebellion, renunciation, revelation, the Cinderella pattern, and many other general types of incidents recur again and again. Most of them are unpleasant, at least at first. Certain more precise situations recur with these: children in queer environments, people in schools, marriages unhappy because loveless, people driven by fear, love affairs between older men and young women, deaths of children, people whose pride is softened or beaten down, and many, many others. Again, the table in Appendix 2 adds some detail to these categories.

Although Dickens uses a large number of types of both characters and incidents, still the mere use of such types would have defeated a less brilliant author. Yet the simple mechanics of Dickens's task were not complete with the packing of installments and the use of stock types. The materials had to be arranged within installments and in patterns attractive to the serial reader in the novel as a whole. Mr. Butt and Mrs. Tillotson, as a result of their study of Dickens's notes and plans, conclude that serial writing, as Dickens did it, "involved maintaining two focuses," "the design and purpose of the novel" and "the identity of the serial number."[13]

This conscious shaping and ordering of the installment can be studied further in Dickens. It is especially interesting in light of the tendency of the serial to end each installment with a climax containing a question left unanswered, a device called a *curtain*. The popular notion is that these are always crude and sensational. As a matter of fact, many novels have dramatic incidents at more or less regular intervals.[14] Naturally such events are exploited in the serial, though not always clumsily. Dickens's serial installments all have structural patterns which use curtains and give evidence of that concern for the order of presentation which Mr. Butt and Mrs. Tillotson demonstrated in Dickens's notes. On the crudest level the serial writer's problem in getting the reader to buy the next installment is mainly one of the order of events. He need not end his installment with a sensation. All he needs are events which the readers will see must have interesting consequences or which are left incomplete in some way. Then he must arrange matters so that such events fall at the ends of installments.

Dickens's installments follow seven basic patterns which do this. Many of the fat installments of Dickens's monthly serials contained several incidents from several plot lines each of which was likely to have interesting results. In installments with this pattern (a), Dickens could end his installment with any of several events. In other cases there were several suitable incidents from one plot line, and the very following of one plot line through several incidents gave the last a special force. With this pattern (b), the problem was only to present incidents enough. Since he wanted his installments to be as pleasing as possible, it was natural that he sometimes arranged the parts of an installment into a pattern with a slow beginning, a middle building up to something, and a climactic end. Of this pattern (c), there were two variations. One (c1) used a single plot thread. The other (c2) used several, merely increasing the pace as the installment proceeded. A fourth pattern (d), involves a surprising and sensational incident at the end of an installment which has consisted of several rather quiet incidents from several plot threads.

These patterns are all too complicated for the leaner installments. The weekly serials (and *Oliver Twist,* which like them appeared in a periodical) tend to have only one or two incidents per installment (rarely more). They usually have one suitable incident and nothing else in the installment (pattern e). Or they have two incidents, from one or two plot threads, of which at least the latter is suitable (pattern f). Or they have two incidents of which the latter is tame, but obviously leads to something interesting (pattern g). A table containing a plot summary example of each of these patterns and listing other examples of each is on pages 201–7 of Appendix 3. Incidentally Mr. Butt and Mrs. Tillotson's editing of the *David Copperfield* notes (in *Dickens at Work,* Chapter VI) makes it clear that in that novel the action in the last chapter of an installment is continued in the first chapter of the next. A study of the novels, installment by installment, shows that this pattern appears in other novels.

The whole matter of the arrangement of installment units was at times seen by Dickens from another

angle. He often thought of the problem of serial publication as one of dividing a rapidly moving story in
the right places. Many letters to the novelists who published in his weekly magazines show this.[15] He thought
of a serial story as primarily one which was easily divided and in one letter he even refused to serialize a
book in his magazine because its tight unity demanded
that it be published *in toto*.[16]

Whatever his angle of vision, Dickens's practice
in writing serial novels certainly involved an element
of mechanical arrangement as he packed his installments, employed stock characters and incidents, and
shaped his installment units. Such fantastic concessions to the serial might seem to have made the creation of great art impossible for him, but he overcame
these difficulties brilliantly.

Chapter 5

A WORLD
IN A BOOK

EVERY CONDITION of serial composition seems almost to have been designed to force an author to become a hack. Moreover, many Victorian authors persisted throughout their careers in writing installments just before they were printed. Of these, Dickens alone succeeded in taming this wilderness of odd conditions concerning arrangement.

His primary method was to turn its disadvantages into advantages by using the disadvantages as a kind of skeleton for his story.

Dickens's deadlines forced a kind of improvisation. So he made freshness and nearly capricious fancy his trademarks.

Dickens's procedure encouraged the use of stock characters. So he selected types which seemed universal to him and then gave them dazzling arrays of peculiarities which reproduced or represented convincingly the individuality of real persons.

His installments required packing with incidents.

So he made up stories with multiple plots and used parallel events and repetitions of character types and situations fugally.

His publication demanded shaped units with forceful conclusions and involved breaks of a week or a month in the initial readings. So he created sensationally vivid pictures of his world which extended beyond any installment unit and swept across all gaps in time.[1]

The structural part of this victory over the problem of serial arrangement is the creation of a fictional world which, while fitting the serial requirements, has also universals and parallels and an ultimate symbolic unity which give that world shape. Let us examine the way in which Dickens gave his fictional world each of these three quantities.

First, if we examine his types of stock characters and incidents more closely, we find that they can be grouped in definite patterns (see Appendix 2) which recur throughout Dickens's novels and are not contradicted. These patterns we may call his universals, in other words. Almost all the characters in Dickens are villains, victims, or rescuers. The villains are so because of avarice, malice, fanaticism, mere femininity, or pride. The victims are maltreated, poor, incapable, or friendless. The rescuers are all clearly shown to be in positions where they can help others. Then the incidents seem to cluster into a pattern which emphasizes being oppressed and escaping. Taken all together, these characters and incidents form a universe of pain and of compensating kindness and excitement. The pain usually involves the bullying and frustrating of the young. The excitement is most often that of gradually coming into one's own. The result is a personal vision which the reader feels at every moment, a vision very different from the worlds of, say, Alexander Pope, or Chaucer, or Stendhal, yet made up of quantities which are universal, which are found in the lives of all of us, and which, in consequence, we recognize as universals at once. Thus the terror of Oliver Twist before Justice Fang and the oppression of Pip at Christmas dinner at the Gargerys' are real and powerful. The typical quality of the orphans does not interfere: Dickens paints forcefully the oppressive action and the reaction of a normal and typical person in the situation.

Second and third, Dickens gave his novels elaborate parallels within their stories and an ultimate symbolic unity. These aspects of each Dickens novel have been discussed together recently. In the development of Dickens's art, however, they appear in two stages. His early novels have a unifying idea and many repetitions and parallels in character and event. They attain a limited unity. The later novels exhibit a thoroughgoing symbolism, in addition, and achieve a profounder unity.

The beginning of unity is in a writer's original view of his book. Fielding had said in Chapter 1 of Book X of *Tom Jones* that every event in the story was related to the aim of the book. Smollett's Preface to *Ferdinand, Count Fathom* echoes this statement. Dickens speaks of *an* idea at the heart of *Oliver Twist, Barnaby Rudge, Martin Chuzzlewit, Dombey and Son, Hard Times, Little Dorrit, A Tale of Two Cities, Great Expectations, Edwin Drood*.[2] By means of such an idea, whether announced or not, he attains in each of his novels, despite his love of variety, a certain narrowing, a selection of detail. Like the events in *Tom Jones*, most of the events in *Pickwick Papers* are related to one idea, the idea of the innocent crusader in a world full of humbug and cheating. This sort of selective thematic unity was the main identity Dickens

gave his early novels. It was a relatively loose as well
as schematic thing. Its oneness was of design and had
a pictorial, spatial,[3] even geometric quality, organized
not around the shape of an action or by means of time
so much as from *fixed* relationships of some kind of
more interest to the author. Forster says *Martin Chuzzlewit* was "to show . . . the number and variety of
humours and vices that have their root in selfishness."[4]

The events in other novels in a similar way are related to themes: the survival of the innocent in a
poisoned environment in *Oliver Twist;* the wickedness
of business in *Nicholas Nickleby;* the crushing of the
innocent by business in *The Old Curiosity Shop;* the
selfish use of religion in *Barnaby Rudge;* the temporary
crushing of love by pride in *Dombey and Son;* the sad-
ness of experience for the unrestrained in *David Copperfield;* the tyranny of Law in *Bleak House;* the crushing of love by economics in *Hard Times;* the prison
which is made of life by the undutiful in *Little Dorrit;*[5]
love and life triumphing over force and death in *A
Tale of Two Cities;* the folly of hope as a way of life in
Great Expectations; the valuelessness of money in *Our
Mutual Friend;* the poisonousness of form without
content in *Edwin Drood.*[6]

This selective thematic kind of unity in Dickens
became much more pronounced after 1840 and came
to be combined with systematic symbolism. These
changes may have been partly caused by the influence
of Carlyle. And then the writing of the Christmas
Books from 1843 to 1847 brought more intense disci-
pline to his creation of plot. Dickens became more conscious of symbolism, and he grew more and more interested in viewing the world through the eyes of a
child (a tendency which will be analyzed later as a
unifier). The new approach added dignity and intensity to his universals and parallel shapes. Only with

this systematic use of symbolism did Dickens finally contain the serial's tendency to encourage mechanical arrangement, for by means of symbolism he now expressed consciously a unified vision of reality which ran through all installments. The development of this symbolism has not been properly examined before, although it occurred at a specific point in Dickens's career. So it is worth detailed discussion. Furthermore, the chronology of the development makes clear the nature of symbolism as Dickens used it. The chronology reveals specifically that for Dickens symbolism was connected with fantasy, with themes urging social reform, and with moral fables for children—perhaps in this way becoming linked to the increasingly biographical tendency in the novels (see Chapter 11).

Dickens had met Carlyle in 1840. Reading Carlyle's works made him more concerned about contemporary conditions. About the beginning of 1844, Forster says, he had become more serious about reform but hopeless that Parliament would do anything about it. At any rate after *A Christmas Carol* (1843), Dickens was out to "convert Society."[7] This statement suggests Dickens had not read Carlyle earlier or had not taken him seriously, but Dickens dedicated *Hard Times* to him and seems to have sought his approval in regard to other works. Mrs. Tillotson suggests that in the 1840's Carlyle taught the English novelists to look at England's social ills as part of a single problem and to convey their views by means of symbols.[8] It seems clear that Dickens was an apt pupil.

Conscious, unified criticism of a whole society (Moslem) is to be found in another of Dickens's sources, James Morier's *The Adventures of Hajji Baba of Ispahan* (1824), mentioned at this time in a letter to Forster. This book emphasizes greed, hypocrisy, and socially and financially competitive selfishness. It also is admittedly modeled on Smollett, much admired by Dickens, and mentions storytelling techniques like the *curtain* in the serial and the "meanderings" spoken of by Dickens (see below) and uses foreshadowing of a kind common in serials.[9]

What has not been perceived, I think, is that Dickens's Christmas Books are the first fruits of these new influences and the vehicles of other pressures also encouraging unity[10] and shaping Dickens's symbolic style. The point seems so obvious once one thinks of it and these works are so familiar that I shall just sketch the consequences for the novels. The Christmas Books were to be published as units and hence demanded greater unity of plot than Dickens had achieved earlier. They employ fantasy. They are shaped so that the stories are parables criticizing certain kinds of individuals (as well as England). They tend to present systematic symbolism in stories which Dickens felt were peculiarly suited to children.

A Christmas Carol was the first and most famous of these five works. In chronology, they overlap with *Martin Chuzzlewit* and *Dombey and Son*. Dickens twice indicates in letters that he has consciously designed a Christmas Book for one reading[16]—the only references directly to the unity of total effect and of construction achieved in these shorter stories, which are without the complexity common in his novels. Perhaps the effort of producing such a unified effect five times caused Dickens to try to pay more attention to overall construction in his later novels. If so, this practice had an effect in line with his resolution after *Martin Chuzzlewit* to *try* to stick to an overall plan more closely.[11] And the novels after *Martin Chuzzlewit* do appear more unified than some of the earlier ones.

Aside from indicating Dickens's drive for greater unity in his works, the Christmas Books reveal tendencies toward the fusion of the real and imaginary and toward the deeper social seriousness mentioned above. Furthermore, more social symbolism is added consciously, though even as early as *Oliver Twist* and *The Old Curiosity Shop* there had been some symbolism.

The fantasy and social symbolism are used together and form the most important development in Dickens's technique aside from the tendency toward an overall effect. Lindsay says that the influence of dream and exaggeration on Dickens's method of composition "reveals its bare bones in many of the short stories."[12] The same could be said of the Christmas Books. In fact Lindsay says that in *A Christmas Carol* "we find the dream method frankly confessed," presumably because the story is to a great extent a series of dreams.[13] The fusion of real and imaginary (here by means of symbolism) and the social seriousness are both indicated in this passage from Forster about Dickens's intentions with regard to the Christmas Books:

No one was more intensely fond than Dickens of old nursery tales [by which term Forster here means mainly Gothic or ghost or supernatural stories], and he had a secret delight in feeling that he was here only giving them a higher form. The social and manly virtues he desired to teach, were to him not less the charm of the ghost, the goblin, and the fairy fancies of his childhood; however rudely set forth in those earlier days. What now were to be conquered were the more formidable dragons and giants that had their places at our own hearths, and the weapons to be used were of a finer than the "ice-Brook's temper." With brave and strong restraints, what is evil in ourselves was to be subdued; with warm and gentle sympathies, what is bad or unreclaimed in others was to be redeemed; the Beauty was to embrace the Beast . . . and we were to play the Valentine with our wilder brothers, and bring them back with brotherly care to civilization and happiness.[14]

Forster adds that he is sure Dickens did do much good.[15] Both fanciful stories and kindness had long been associated with Christmas; it was perhaps only natural to join the two. Dickens himself said the books were to have effects like those of masques or morality plays[16] (yet he got angry at Cruikshank, who crudely adopted fairy tales to the cause of temperance).[17]

A general interest in symbolism and symbolic teaching is noticeable from this time on in Dickens. The article about Cruikshank is one evidence. It states that fairy stories are good teachers of virtue to children and that they should not be altered by an individual to suit his "opinions"; they are wrecked if this is done.[18] A little before writing *David Copperfield*, Dickens wrote that he could not write a farce because he was " 'constantly striving, for' " his " 'reputation's sake, to get into it a meaning that is impossible in a farce.' "[19] In 1850 he wrote two articles about popular melodramas. In one melodrama he noted the "confusion between right and wrong."[20] He was worried about the lack of seriousness in most melodramas. He says he "would decidedly interpose to turn to some wholesome account the means of instruction which it has at command." "It would not be exacting much, or exacting anything very difficult, to require that the pieces represented in these theatres should have, at least, a good, plain, healthy purpose in them." Dickens's cure is interesting—apparently largely preaching and reformed plots.[21]

He even wrote a vigorously symbolic play. While he was writing the last installments of *Little Dorrit,* the novel which contains the openly symbolic fantasy of the Circumlocution Office, Forster says, Dickens was writing in collaboration with Collins a play called *The Frozen Deep.*[22] It involves a rescue in the Arctic of a young man by an older man who loves the same girl and eventually renounces her. Lindsay says that according to the prologue Dickens saw the "north as a symbol of the inner landscape."[23] In this connection it is interesting that Forster says that the play was being prepared for the Dickens children to give. Here is another hint of that curious association between that which is fit for children and that which is systematically symbolic, which we saw in Forster's comment about nursery tales reworked for Christmas Books earlier. Perhaps Dickens felt the moral reform of an individual restored him to childish innocence and hence associated moralistic symbolism with children (the novels with an autobiographical method appeared after the Christmas Books). Or perhaps he simply found this kind of moral fable common in works intended for children. At any rate he had always liked this kind of story, and Carlyle's work gave it new meaning and intellectual respectability.

Finally the folktale analogues mentioned in connection with *Great Expectations* by Mr. Stange[24] and the general fairy-tale atmosphere of *Great Expectations*, which makes the happy ending at least half suitable despite its contradiction of the plot, remind one of the Christmas Books and *The Frozen Deep* in regard to the symbolic rewriting of nursery stories for a higher purpose.

Mrs. Tillotson notes the constant use of the house and firm symbols in *Dombey and Son,* and the symbolism of the church scenes, all suggesting, she feels, that "house, firm, and church" are "three hollow shells of the established order."[25] But it is not until *Bleak House* that Dickens succeeded in organizing virtually a whole novel in considerable detail symbolically. And this novel is largely social criticism. Thereafter all his novels are organized in this way. In *Bleak House* the house, fog, law, sickness, and death imagery are very detailed, and sometimes suggestions are made by means of symbols about the importance of facts or events. The law is "connected" with the government of Coodle and Doodle, the religion of Chadband, the poverty of the brickmakers, the madness of Miss Flite, the fantastic spontaneous combustion of Krook, and hundreds of other things. The law by means of settling the lives of all of these people is part of the triviality of the aristocracy and the discomfort of the poor.

Forster says of the *plot* construction in a commentary which has been widely imitated:

In his *later* writings he *had been* [my italics] assiduously cultivating this essential of his art, and here he brought it very nearly to perfection. Of the tendency of composing a story piecemeal to induce greater concern for the part than the whole, he had been always conscious; but I remember a remark also made by him to the effect that to read a story in parts had no less a tendency to prevent the readers' noticing how thoroughly a work so presented might be calculated for perusal as a whole. Look back from the last to the first page of the present novel, and not even in the highest examples of this kind of elaborate care will it be found that event leads more closely to event, or that the separate incidents have been planned with a more studied consideration of the bearing they are severally to have on the general result. Nothing is introduced at random, everything tends to the catastrophe, the various lines of plot converge and fit to its centre, and to the larger interest all the rest is irresistibly drawn. The heart of the story is a Chancery suit. On this the plot hinges; and on incidents connected with it, trivial or important, the passion and suffering turn exclusively. Chance words, or the deeds of chance people, to appearance irrelevant, are found everywhere influencing the course taken by a train of incidents of which the issue is the life or death, happiness or misery, to men and women perfectly unknown to them. . . . [all sorts of legal and financial characters] are forever moving around the lives of the chief persons in the tale, and drawing them on insensibly, but very certainly, to the issues that await them. Even the fits of the little law-stationer's servant help *directly* in the chain of small things that lead *indirectly* [my italics] to Lady Dedlock's death. One strong chain of interest holds together [all the groups of characters and the places they frequent]. . . . The characters multiply as the tale advances, but in each the *drift* is the same [my italics]. . . .[26]

Even in his early novels, then, Dickens gave some shape to his novels by means of universal character and incident patterns, parallels, and thematic selection of material. In the 1840's, however, he developed a new technique of systematic symbolism which was associated with other tendencies in his art, such as his fondness for fantasy, his social seriousness, and his interest in moral fables for children. This new symbolism became the basis of a really successful containment of the disintegrative forces in the serial.

POLARITY AND
ARRANGEMENT WITHIN
TIME IN THE NOVEL

A STRUCTURAL SCHEME by itself may be enough for a
philosophical or sociological or psychological treatise
but the novelist gives us both a scheme and a detailed
picture of a familiar world. We expect therefore to see
his scheme work because we expect him to make us
pass through an experience of reality itself. To move
us through an experience, the novelist gives us a sense
of the organizations of people, things, groups, and ab-
stractions and involves them in a progression of observable events through time. Thus the novelist assumes that a world of external organizations and movements exists and that we can be brought to know it.
His assumptions contradict much of modern philosophy, but the fact that readers so often feel he succeeds
in such an attempt suggests that the experience of most
people may not support the philosophers' formal theories of knowledge, or more properly, of ignorance.

The organizations of people and objects are themselves organized by the novelist in a simple polarity. This polarity and the progression of events involving it are easy to see working independently alongside the pervasive metaphor. They are a way of answering one of the most fundamental questions the individual asks of life or a novel: "What is happening?" The question is essentially a person's attempt to discover where he is within time as well as space. It is a more complex and abstract question than "Where am I?" since it assumes that "Where am I?" can be answered, and answered differently at different points in time. So a more complex process is required to find its answer. To answer "Where am I?" the person tries to get an overall geographic view and then compares his place with the whole, but to answer "What is happening, or where am I within place and time?" he makes a series of observations and comparisons.

The objection may be made that in Chapter 3 I sketched one process of orientation or acquiring knowledge and that here I am describing a totally different process and contending that it too is orientation. "Are not novelists and their readers aware," the skeptic may ask, "that orientation or acquiring knowledge is one thing, one process?" I must protest that we learn in different ways in different situations and that my examples of orientation are true and separate types drawn from life itself. Looking at the world from the top of a mountain, one could answer the question "What is happening?" as well as the question "Where am I?" but the Olympian life is notoriously slow-moving for all its virtues of other kinds.

It is easier to understand the progression involving a polarity, this second characteristic meaning of orientation, in new contexts. Let us consider a situation in which one naturally tries to find out "What is happening?" Suppose one is walking along a street. Suddenly he hears cries. They come from an alley behind a restaurant. There he sees a husky young sailor wrestling with a hatchet-faced, white-haired man in the thin white jacket and white paper hat of a dishwasher. The dishwasher is yelling. The sailor drags his opponent down and begins to beat him with his fists. The observing individual runs over to break up the fight. The sailor shouts, "Try to take my wallet when I'm puking sick in the washroom will you?" and becoming wild, takes off a shoe and hammers the dishwasher's head. The observer grabs the sailor's arm and the dishwasher's and tells the sailor to make his complaint to the police.

Now, I ask you, where in this incident does the observer know what is happening or what his role will be? He gets the overall picture of a fight at once, but he has only a fuzzy idea of it at first. Then the matter begins to clear and he has a general idea: one man is beating the other. His view must become more and more specific, however, before he can answer the question satisfactorily. This is the kind of process the novelist tries to set up.

A complete answer may of course be impossible, but the human being naturally seeks some answer because of anxiety, curiosity, pity, or some other immediate emotional assessment of the situation's relation to the whole of his life. Essentially the individual's sense of what is happening, of where he is within place and time, is not acquired quickly—unlike his feeling of where he is, which the individual tries to determine at once. Furthermore, in order to tell what is happening, the individual must seek differences and similarities in detail both in place and time. By itself, as one fact within space, the fight mentioned above is of limited use: when the individual observer compares it quickly with his life as a whole, he can come to the conclusion "this fight is a terrible thing" or "this fight is a frightening thing" or "this fight is what I would expect in this part of town" or others—depending on the nature of his life as a whole. Only when he compares it to another detail, another point in time, that is, the absence of a fight a moment before, does he have even the vaguest idea of the nature of the fight: it has just begun. He must then seek other comparisons in detail between various points in time and place. One man begins to overcome the other; one man accuses the other of a crime; one man becomes frenzied and brutal. It is only by comparing the situation and behavior of one man to those of the other several times and by comparing one moment to another several times that the observing individual in this case can determine that the sailor is furiously taking the law into his own hands and can calculate his own role in the incident.

He has needed a series of comparisons. He has needed the differences within place, which have indicated the facts at any one moment, and the differences within time, which have indicated movement or change. He has needed the similarities within place at different points in time: it is the winner who accuses; it is the winner who accuses who becomes frenzied. He has needed also the similarities in time or coincidences: as he wins, the sailor becomes more excited. These similarities indicate the meaning of the facts and the direction of the movement.

There is nothing unusual in the observer's procedure in this instance. Suppose we are standing in a meadow and want to find out which way the wind is blowing. On a cold day it may seem to be coming from all directions. We may look at the long grass. We find that the grass, which normally grows upward, has been bent sideways. We think perhaps that this is a spot where a farm animal has lain down; so we look at other spots. If we can see that in many places the grass is bent in the same direction, we can determine which way the wind is moving. Again the observer in order to locate movement must find points of difference and of conflict between forces. Then, in order to determine its direction, he must also find some similarity or consistency between points. On television an announcer will try to give us a sense of what is happening concerning the weather, a war, a flood, etc., by showing maps and diagrams; by reporting on what was true yesterday, this morning at six, in midafternoon; by indicating high and low pressure areas, hot and cold air masses, concentrations of opposing troops, dikes, water heights; by sketching movements and showing directions. Information about the stock market from magazines, tapes, or personal sources tends to present very similar kinds of things. The question "What is happening?" in situations involving obvious conflict and in others lacking it leads the individual naturally, then, to a polarization of view in which there are sides and he seeks to characterize the sides and measure the progress of one over the other. The question moreover demands a prolonged use of the senses and a certain cold intellectual calculation as well as the rapid emotional assessment called for by the easier question "Where am I?"

The novelist tries to guide a similar process by supplying data. The question "What is happening?" can neither be asked nor answered without movement. The reading of page after page of any book about individual people suggests movement. Hence though he may not wish to (as E. M. Forster notes of Gertrude Stein), the novelist is forced to recognize that the reader will ask the question, and forced to supply in some measure the polarization with a progress which answers the question and helps the reader organize the vast mass of detail in his book. Some authors attempt to substitute the periodic introduction of sadistic or pornographic sensation, but this does not work very well. Occasionally an author produces a novel like Joyce's *Ulysses*, which has a basic metaphorical and mythical pattern executed in great detail, but is so slow and thorough and predictable in its working out that it seems to lack movement and ends by being dull. The very, very slow or the completely predictable seems the same and unchanged. So, to get the full effect of recognized and charted movement, a novel must have some rapidity and a certain amount of surprise (and incompleteness or mystery) as well as an actual polarization with a progress.

While we may not be used to thinking of the novelist as telling us what is happening by supplying us with a polarity and a progression in it, the process is nevertheless familiar as a means of teaching and learning. Yet the widely respected theory of Hume declares that any such orientation is impossible. Our knowledge of the external world and of our feelings, it is said, is all by means of a stream of internal, simple, atomized sensations and therefore we can have no knowledge of shapes either in an exterior world or in ourselves. It may be most sensible to say that such a view is a bit too severe in its contemptuous defining away of our mental powers. Merely by tracing internal sensations we can reach ideas which encourage our common-sense approach to answering the question "What is happening?"

Let us imagine ourselves going through the experiences of a baby and see how this is true. We note that sensations are of different kinds. They are also of differing degrees of complexity. The simple pain from a pinpoint starts as a mere spot, but we identify and locate it mainly by quick contrast with sensations from other parts of the body. The view of a whole room is different, for it instantly gives us notions of shapes and relationships. The view may be defined as one manifold sensation or as the occurrence all at once of millions of little ones locked into an arrangement. It does not matter; it is complex in either case. By tracing sensations, we can discover changes within time in the form of various different repeated sequences of sensations. The human being has several senses all operating at once, but we can also discover different repeated sequences proceeding from the operation of one sense organ, the ears, say, or the eyes. We feel that most sensations, especially painful ones, have reference to the world outside ourselves, and of course the organs recording these sensations are mostly located on the outside of the body. Many complex sensations are accompanied by, and many sequences end with, a distinct sensation of identification or control. We are moved to accept the idea because we often, though not always, find that a sequence of simple sensations is consistent with a single complex, millionfold sensation or because two separate senses supply us with consistent sequences. So from our installment-like sensations we form notions of shapes and space, of movements and time in a world exterior to ourselves.

We experience some sequences and sensations with pleasure, others with pain. We find that some can be produced at will, others not. In both cases we notice that certain sequences and notions of the exterior world are associated with pleasure and control or with pain and helplessness. By controlled movements of the body we find that we can increase some pleasurable sensations and decrease some painful ones; that is, we can decide upon a sequence of movements and sensations and then behave so that this same pattern occurs consistently. So we conclude that we know a reality external to us because we learn to feed ourselves and to walk without bumping into furniture. We can verify the idea that this working partnership is indeed knowledge by putting one hand over our ear or cheek and using one internal set of sensations to check the validity of another set's picture of the shape of something external to it. Ultimately the consistency of our sensations among themselves and with those spoken of by other people is what proves that our senses produce knowledge, and it is a fair test, for consistency is the philosophic test which is commonly applied to all theory. I should add that logic involves a simultaneous consistency within space. The empirical consistency of which I have spoken is a consistency within time, but does not for that reason cease to be consistency.

Let us not be deterred, then, by quibbles from respecting what we observe in the novel. A situation is set up in which we are led to ask "What is happening?" and a polarity and a progression in it are supplied to lead us to an answer. The polarity usually involves the struggle of an individual against a problem (as in *Pamela* and *Manon Lescaut*), the struggle of one or more individuals against an environment (as in *Vanity Fair* and *Middlemarch*), or the struggle of a conflict-torn individual against a conflict-torn society (as in *The Red and the Black* and *Notes from Underground*). Such a battling is more than the simple conflict to be found in all stories. In dramas, epics, and romances the conflicts are more public, the lines of battle are much less clear, and the minor characters often straddle the conflict altogether. Besides, in the novel, another element usually is developed in order to underline the polarity. Watt rightly suggests that the love story is much commoner in the novel than in most other forms and has been a sort of signature of the novel. The significance of these facts is that there are partnerships in the novel as well as antagonisms, and the novel tends to have regular teams or sides as well as a protagonist and an antagonist. The lovers and the antagonisms are usually related. The lovers may be antagonists as well, as in *Victory* and *Jane Eyre*. Or both may seem to be on one side in a sort of Romeo-and-Juliet relation as in *The Cloister and the Hearth* or *The Sorrows of Young Werther*, but this latter relationship is rarer. Love is so central to many novels that the polarity in them is between lover-antagonists and the progress is from greater antagonism to more love or vice versa or some combination. Where the progress is not in love, it is usually in man's relation to his environment or a force or forces behind it, as in *Pilgrim's Progress, Robinson Crusoe, Tom Jones, Roderick Random, Waverley, The Way of All Flesh, Man's Fate, Stalingrad.* In such novels either minor characters are introduced as members of one side or the other, or virtually all the characters are given equal weight and are on one side—that of man against his environment.

Now obviously this polarity in a novel overlaps with the pervasive metaphorical system, but it is not the same thing. The metaphor of marriage pervades *Middlemarch*. The polarity in that novel is the struggle of several individuals with their environment. This war with environment is one of the relationships symbolized in the novel in marriage (as also varieties of characters are symbolized there by varieties of marital choice and experience). But the thing symbolized and the symbol itself are different. The first is a device itself (of organization) on one level while the symbol or metaphor is another device deliberately elaborated to picture the first, among other things. A few polarities run through almost all novels, but hundreds of symbols have been used to explain them. A polarity is a narrow-ing of forces and requires narrowing of observation. A symbol by its very nature tends toward elaboration in every direction.

The connection of the progression to the basic metaphor in a novel is even slighter. Any one event can easily be related to a metaphorical scheme. The rates at which events occur, however, and the se-quences of events, while having a general significance within such a scheme by indicating some quality of the metaphoric world's order, are often developed in great detail. In fact they form one of the chief causes of excitement and interest in some novels, perhaps even most. This development is out of all proportion to the symbolic significance.

Furthermore, the progression is closely connected to that level of the novel which is taken as direct and literal reality. It is a direct imitation, not a symbolic substitution. It conveys a sense of the speed and strength of forces in reality and hence is an important expression of the author's sense of reality. In a way the metaphorical system suggests a pattern of gen-eralizations while the progression is concerned with living, moving example. The progression, then, is an independent form of organization in the novel which helps orient and satisfy the individual in a different way.

The progression is temporal not spatial, and de-spite the common belief that time is like space, the in-dividual in many temporal relationships behaves and feels differently from the way he does in spatial ones. Within space, an individual wants to know where he is. The pervasive metaphor provides a rather external geography, a network of relationships, a unified world he can see (Mr. Rahv goes so far as to suggest that myth is actually a denial of time, in *The Myth and the Powerhouse*, New York, 1965, pp. 3–21). Within time, the individual feels himself involved in conflict in a moving world of many things, for the sense of time is an awareness of motion and fades if motion disappears for long. Instead of trying to see his world merely as organized or attempting merely to organize it, as in the grasping at a pervasive metaphor, he tries to see his world cut up, as Bergson suggests, or attempts to split it into the stages of a mechanical progression involving a polarity. Within time, he wants to move, to split his world, to take sides, to rearrange objects, to win, and to know what is happening, who are the antagonists, and who is winning. His involvement in conflict implies external organizations and changes. So he searches for measurements of these things as independent quantities. When orienting himself in relation to both space and time, he tries to combine these different explorations into a pattern which makes sense.

Yet conflicts and strengths and timing are rather abstract. So he cannot see them and within time must feel his way toward a sense of them by a sort of internal assessment of his own reactions to sensational stimuli. The novelist using this tendency makes as plain as he can the differences and similarities in situation for some individual character in his novel at different points in time in order to indicate the progress which these differences and similarities compose. The reader is usually brought to sympathize with one principal character or with one group (one pole) and is led to feel the polarity and the progress as this protagonist does, though perhaps in a way modified by various balancing points of view. In this way the author can make use of the individual's tendency to seek points of difference and similarity and his tendency to follow the patterns they form which answer the question "What is happening, or where am I in time and space?"

The reader can trace this splitting, choosing of sides, seeking of measurement in progression, etc., in the examples from experience given above and in the extended example from fiction which will be presented shortly. Yet another widely accepted theory, that of Kant, would deny the possibility of such behavior by picturing knowing as mostly organizing and by largely excluding movement from the process. This theory of knowledge is dominated by the notions of the unity of consciousness and of the existence of a gap between that unity and an independent world outside it. Man, it is said, has sensational reactions, but his feelings of their origins are contaminated by the admixture of himself. Space and time are merely such human forms added to the raw material. What man represents to himself, phenomena, are many, and the imagination, by means of symbols, organizes them into twelve categories which are themselves organized permanently in relation to the unity of consciousness. The phenomena can be distinguished and arranged mechanically on a lower level by the senses and the understanding, but the higher levels of knowledge and the shapes seen by the imagination, are organic or plant-like, as are the categories, which are specifically called seeds. Like the idea of the narrowness of sensational knowledge, this view tends to belittle the extent to which an individual can be informed or directed by contact with the world outside of him.

If we reflect a little, we find that there are difficulties with parts of this organizational theory. When taken account of, these indicate that we should modify the conclusions considerably. First, much of this theory depends upon weak spots in the earlier one. Second, the unity of a consciousness being fed mountains of data by several different senses and the notion of a single pattern of knowing are not consistent with human experience. Third, the quick dismissal of time and space is eccentric, since they form much of any body of knowledge and since all learning and knowing processes involve changes within time. Fourth, it is, moreover, illogical to say time and space are fixed internal forms of the mind but then in developing a description of an internal process of knowing not to include further discussion and analysis of them. Obviously, the dismissal of time and space then was only an attempt to destroy confidence in empirical knowledge and to make room for this unconsciously spatial theory with its distinct slanting in favor of an anti-material, *a priori*, idealized view. Fifth, we must note another internal contradiction in this theory. Phenomena are different or they would all fit into one category. The sources of these differences may be within the mind or external or both, but if they are not external in source, the world and mind could come together at once and the gap would disappear. So they must be external. Therefore, since differences in nature are in some sense differences of shape or arrangement, logically the mind must be able to distinguish shapes external to it although the theory has expressly denied this.

The fundamental problem here is that the theory excludes conflict and movement in the mind, but in life organizing is accompanied by disorganizing and unity by division, at least in the form of distinguishing of differences. So one cannot relegate distinguishing difference and seeing mechanical relations to one level and raise organic unifying to another: they go on together. Moreover, in life organizing is accompanied by being organized, and influences are mutual. Environmental creation of moods, pain, and some behavior are as obvious as subjective arrangement of data. So one cannot sensibly picture knowledge as one-sided. The failure to account for these truths led to a theoretical process of knowing which fails to seem operative and seems parallel to no remembered mental process.

We need have no philosophic hesitations, then, about accepting tentatively the empirically derived suggestion that in a situation within time we seek to find out what is happening by mentally splitting the world we see, choosing sides, seeking measurement in progression, and so on. The novelist makes use of these processes as we can see in Smollett's *Humphry Clinker*. At first this novel seems like an exception to the proposition that there is a polarity and a progress in each novel. It is written in letters composed mainly by five major characters. Their personalities and views are very different, and all we seem to have are miscellaneous pictures of events and places on a journey they are taking, the journey itself appearing to go in no specific direction. There is a good deal of social satire of the life at Bath, of the characters themselves, of London, of various people they meet; and there is considerable leisurely conversation. No obvious action and no simple melodrama hero and villain appear.

Yet a clear polarity emerges quickly. One character, Matthew Bramble, gets most of the space. He is also the most forceful, most experienced, most sensitive, and most intelligent of the characters. It is soon clear that this cantankerous, rational, hypersensitive, educated, hypochondriacal old Welsh country gentleman is both by his social position and by personal nature the leader of the little group of travelers. That group consists of his ingenuous and romantic niece; his bland college student nephew; his shrewish, sex-starved, provincial, middle-aged sister; and her ignorant, ambitious, blunt, half-unconscious maidservant. Matthew's hypochondria and his discomfort at the noise, dirt, and absurdity of Bath are loudly and vigorously expressed. Also an explosive collision between him and his sister Tabitha occurs over his charity to a widow there. The same hard-soft duality of his character is borne out by later incidents also, such as his restraint of his sister in order to spare the others and his denunciation of London while he tolerantly lets his niece amuse herself at social gatherings there. Again and again it is the disorderly in London, Tabitha, Humphry's Methodist preaching, and so on which arouses his hard critical side. Equally we see that his pity and sympathy are extended when he finds the needs of other people. In those incidents which call forth his comments, the censoriousness becomes less and less angry irritation and more and more intelligent analysis with speculation as to cures and causes. His sympathy seems to broaden. Experience of the world outside of himself and visiting varied but ideally ordered parts of Scotland, which Matthew actually admires, mellow and cure Matthew. At the end of the novel, when he returns home and completes his geographically circular journey, he has found an outlet for his orderly intelligence and aggressiveness in helping his friend order his estate. He has found another outlet in arranging the marriages and future security of his less experienced niece and of the wildly instinctive people, his sister and her maidservant. He has fused his personal sympathy and his general rationalism and his instinctive aggressiveness. He has unified himself.

We begin dazzled by the intensity and variety of the novel's pictures and incidents, but we quickly find our attention drawn to Matthew's powerful but mixed feelings about the world about him. We follow the changing proportions of his hatred and love until geographically he has come back to where he started, but emotionally he has reversed his proportions and reached rest, both from journeying and from fighting against his world. We can feel in sequence that we are at the start, in the middle, and at the end of a battle. The chief metaphorical pattern in this book is a complex fusion of a journey-growth to a real home and healthy interaction with others. Metaphors of architecture and sex and violence are subordinated to this central image pattern. While virtually every detail in the novel is related to this basic metaphor, we can as easily relate the same details to the overlapping organization by polarity. There is hardly anything in the novel which does not become related to Matthew's passionate feeling toward his environment and his struggle to order and to merge with it. The chamberpots, the tortures of American Indians, the teeth of Tabby's dog, the unconscious misspelling of words by the two uneducated females, Matt's sudden praise of his home in the country after he has been exposed to London, the highwayman (reluctantly a fairly complete outlaw) —all are tied to Matt's battle.

The progression in *Humphry Clinker* has indicated to us what the polarity within the novel is and how it was moving; it has made easy and pleasant the reading of a book which at first looked forbidding. We have enjoyed identifying ourselves with Matt and engaging in his fight and love affair with his environment (of course there is also the elaborate metaphorical scheme to help the reader). The question "What is happening?" is answered in a general way fairly early in some novels, but to the very end we go on asking the question at least in relation to details. Then the sense of the present time is very strong and the question "What is happening?" remains insistent and every answer helps satisfy us. As a result perhaps we tend to look to the metaphorical system for instruction and to the progression for pleasure in the novel. We may object to some of the progression, to some of the answers to our question. For example, the marriage of Matt Bramble's niece seems hurried and not wholly prepared for (within the timing and progression—it may make perfect sense within the metaphorical scheme and still not work in the progression). The marriage of Tabitha and the change in Matt, however, are believable in pace and sequence and hence contribute to our identification with Matt and his progress.

We have observed now that a metaphorical system cannot be equated with a novel. We have seen that the variety and enigmatic nature of the novel are reflections of the quality of individual life. Muir's *Structure of the Novel* (1929) described novels emphasizing space or time, but went little beyond that. We, however, have traced the individual's need of orientation in space and time and have seen the operation of metaphor and progression as two of the novelist's means of supplying that orientation in his work. There are undoubtedly other problems of orientation and other methods of simultaneous organization of the novel. Yet I believe the sketch given here of these two is enough to suggest that the novel, like an ellipse or other complex geometric shape, is a unity developed around at least two foci and not a simple figure like a circle or a starfish. One implication of this idea is that several kinds of criticism can be helpful. For example, Aristotelian plot criticism can be combined with the New Critics' metaphorical approach.

In Dickens, the problem of the reader's wondering "What is happening or where am I in time as well as space?" was magnified by his being able to read only a small part of the story at any one time and having long intervals between parts. Indeed it was intensified so much that the problem of progression and the problem of polarity became partly split. We have seen that every novelist faces the problem of arrangement within portions of his story and that the arrangement is geographic placing at the microscopic level. Similarly, arrangement within time is the form taken by the setting up of a progression at the microscopic level. Now, the novel form is such that one description or narration or dialogue follows another; so the reader has some sense of arrangement in time even if the author does no such arranging. The serial encouraged Dickens as we have seen, to make the installments into story units. The next chapter will show how it further encouraged him to see events as mere beads on a string, since the reader got the second installment a month after the first and the third a month after the second and hence had a minimal sense of progression from the mere purchasing in sequence. A result of this was the temptation merely to extend one or more plot lines a little way but aimlessly. On the other hand, the very slowness of one's reading of a serial intensified the need for a sense of progression. It so happens that Dickens believed in a rather disorderly world and in a basic passivity in sympathetic human beings. Such polarity as he saw in life, then, took the pattern of a sensitive being pushed about in a hurly-burly. In consequence, he could persuade himself at times that what might seem meaningless, separate, varied little events happening to a passive protagonist were art and truth, however crude the procedure might seem to the reader. A large number of events in a full installment could by itself thus seem to Dickens like movement and the passage of time seen in a very simple way.

Chapter 8 will show, however, that needing a sense of design between installments and within time, he pushed to more complex and more definite patterns. He set up markedly contrasting teams of characters and alternating plots and sequences. He developed the ability to inform the reader impressionistically by means of contrasts and parallels in details of situation, description, behavior. He added a specific mystery which was gradually both made more intense and unraveled. He used the technique of arousing suspense so systematically that in the middle and late novels even paragraphs and chapters within individual installments are governed by the mystery. While he developed these methods of suggesting polarity and progression, he also usually set up a polarity between an aggressive villain connected with a mystery or an oppressing, mysterious environment and a passive protagonist. In Dickens this latter aspect of polarity is so tightly related to the psychological continuity of the novels because the protagonists are passive that I shall defer until my last chapter illustration of what, in Dickens at least, is the rather obvious matter of actually naming the poles involved.

One complex aspect of polarity, however, must and will be discussed in close connection with progression in Chapter 8. Since Dickens's protagonists were usually passive, the polarity to a large extent consisted of, or was strongly associated with, differences in places which acted as stimuli upon the protagonist. Thus, intense symbolism of place, the solution to Dickens's first serial problem, became combined with his extreme, even weirdly melodramatic, polarity. The protagonist tended to move between two places in Dickens's novels (as in *A Tale of Two Cities*), one of which became associated with symbols of evil and another which became a final haven, sought more and more eagerly. Thus Dickens's particular view of man and life led him almost to separate progression and polarity in a way. But his view brought him to portray a progression in general knowledge in relation to some specific, and a development in the protagonist's happiness which re-merged progression and polarity.

THE SERIAL'S
DEMAND FOR ADVANCE

As we have seen, serial publication suggested some plot movement, yet produced an intensified need for it. The audience had to feel that the story was going somewhere, that each installment contained one or more advances in plot. To communicate a sense of advance or progression, an author must so arrange his materials that one segment of story read after another will contain certain basic quantities found in the first, but also differences or contrasts, and segments read still later will extend these differences until a recognizable change in the polar basic quantities is seen complete. Especially in a story with many plot lines and characters, the author has considerable choice about the order of events. The problem of polarity and progression here is another problem of arrangement—in a line or lines and, in terms of the story world, an arrangement in time.

Again, as in the matter of spatial arrangement, the serial, especially at first, tempted Dickens to arrange materials with a kind of mechanical efficiency.

In this case it encouraged him to overlook the need for fixed poles and create advance for its own sake or directionless advance. This chapter will describe the problem briefly. Later I will discuss his solutions.

Some of Dickens's remarks about plotting indicate his attitudes and through them the ways in which serials tended to push him. In the 1837 Preface to the completed *Pickwick Papers,* he said in part:

it was necessary—or it appeared so to the author—that every number should be to a certain extent, complete in itself, and yet that the whole twenty numbers, when collected, should form one tolerably harmonious whole, each leading to the other by a gentle and not unnatural progress of adventure.[1]

Ten years later, by which time he had written seven novels of his fifteen, he said: "It was observed, in the Preface to the original Edition, that the Pickwick Papers were designed for the introduction of diverting characters and incidents; that no ingenuity of plot was attempted, or even at that time considered very feasible by the author in connection with the desultory mode of publication adopted; and that the machinery of the Club proving cumbrous in the management, was gradually abandoned, as the work progressed." A little later in the same 1847 Preface he said, "Experience and study have since taught me something, and I could perhaps wish now, that these chapters were strung together on a stronger thread of general interest, still, what they are, they were designed to be."[2]

What is interesting here is that progression, but not ingenuity of plot, seemed right to him for his first serial and that the simple idea of incidents arranged like beads on a string is still his view of the problem of progression as late as the middle of his career.

During the composition of his eighth novel, *David*

Copperfield, he made a remark which suggests the operation of this idea. He wrote to Forster as he composed the third installment. " 'I feel, thank God, quite confident in the story. I have a move in it ready for this month; another for next; and another for the next.' "[3]

In practice, he advanced one or more parts of the plot a little way in every installment. In *Bleak House* for instance, in the fifth installment (a), Richard starts work in medicine and begins to think of the possibility of the law suit's prospering (a hope to which he later clings with great tenacity, allowing himself to play at several careers—a hope which, when finally frustrated, kills him). In the same installment (b), Esther (the heroine) meets her future husband, Woodcourt. Also (c), Jarndyce meets Neckett's children, one of whom he later hires as his ward Esther's maid. She gives Esther smallpox, and this sickness contributes to the plot in various ways; for instance, it makes Lady Dedlock's revelation that she is Esther's mother less important. Finally in the same monthly part (d), Lady Dedlock in disguise asks Jo (the sweeper) about a dead man's grave. The dead man was her fiancé and was Esther's father, it later turns out. Also Jo is one of the means by which Tulkinghorn is able to discover Lady Dedlock's secret, a discovery which brings about her death and his own.

The ideas of sketches, of beads on a string, or of mere advances in plot lines are open-ended, somewhat directionless. There is considerable evidence that as a result Dickens found his plots appearing, turning, and ending in ways which surprised him.

Two books were begun as serials before he knew he was going to develop novels out of them: *Pickwick Papers* began as a series of sketches, as we saw above, and *The Old Curiosity Shop* began as an idea for a serialized story of "a short half-dozen chapters."[4] Two other novels began as writings which were halted and redirected before they reached the public: *David Copperfield* began as a confidential autobiographical fragment,[5] and *Great Expectations* began as a pictorial sketch which was to be one of the romantic, half-serious, frequently reminiscent articles in *All the Year Round*.[6]

There were also extraordinary breaks in structure, and changes in the general nature of Dickens's books. Examples of these are everywhere. As Dickens admits in his Preface, the second half of *Pickwick Papers* is more serious than the first.[7] Forster says of *The Old Curiosity Shop* that "its very incidents created a necessity at first not seen [but pointed out by Forster]; and it was carried to a close only contemplated after a full half of it was written [and most of this part published]."[8]

Of *Martin Chuzzlewit*, which began with the idea about Pecksniff, Forster says, "Beginning so hurriedly as at last he did, altering his course at the opening and seeing little yet of the main track of his design, perhaps no story was ever begun by him with stronger heart or confidence."[9] Earlier Forster had said that "the work became modified, in its progress, by changes at first not contemplated; but as early [!] as the third number he drew up the plan of 'old Martin's plot to degrade and punish Pecksniff,' and the difficulties he encountered in departing from other portions of his scheme were such as to render him, in subsequent stories, more bent upon constructive care at the outset, and on adherence so far as might be to any design he had formed." In his Preface Dickens assured his readers that he " 'had endeavored to resist the temptation of the current Monthly Number, and to keep a steadier eye upon the general purpose and design.' "[10] There were other additions, too. Because of poor sales, Dickens announced at the end of the fourth number that one of the characters was going to America.[11] Moreover, he invented Sarah Gamp after seven numbers (or about a third of the novel) were written.[12]

His resolution to do more planning made a difference, but it did not always and altogether control Dickens. Despite the developed *structural* contrasts between Dora and Agnes in *David Copperfield,* Dickens hesitated long about whether Dora should die.[13] In *Hard Times* the symbolic contrast between "economic" man and the circus world of make-believe is only visible at the start and the end of the book. Sissy Jupe is clearly dropped after a beginning which virtually promises a story about her. The book passes instead to the world of Stephen, Louisa, and Bounderby. And even in this story Dickens was a bit unsure of his structure. Mr. Butt and Mrs. Tillotson tell us that Dickens seemed to have "some doubt of the final issue of Louisa's actions."[14] In regard to *Little Dorrit,* the speculator Sadleir, on whom Dickens said he based Merdle, committed suicide after Dickens had written the beginning of the book,[15] and Dickens, during the composition of the seventh number, spoke of having at last " 'resolved to make Dorrit rich [in the tenth number].' "[16] Then, too, says Forster, Dickens worked hard (but admittedly failed) to connect Miss Wade's story with the main plot, even studying the inserted stories in Fielding and Smollett to try to get help.[17]

Finally the well-known changed ending to *Great Expectations* indicates a weak feeling for the plot direction. And his doubts about *Edwin Drood's* structure and pace suggest something similar.

Another effect of the serial's inexorable demand for progression is the creation of loose ends. Dickens sometimes just wrote about unrelated characters and events (especially in the first half of a novel) and related them to earlier material at his leisure. Flintwich's twin in *Little Dorrit* is an example of a loose end which only got tied up at the last minute. His appearance is the sensation of Chapter IV, the last in the first installment. Other (but more completely unrelated) loose ends are Pet's twin in *Little Dorrit*, the visit to Fagin's death cell in *Oliver Twist*, Darnay's trial for treason in England, and Orlick's deeds of violence in *Great Expectations*. Clearly Dickens often relied on his memory of previous installments as he wrote, and his memory was not always perfect. The penalty was the unexpected disadvantage of the loose-end method: bits which never got woven into the rest of the story.

Various other inconsistencies in the novels are probably traceable to the same cause, some perhaps in part explained by Dickens's simply forgetting what character he had once given the doer of a certain action or what previous actions he had done. For instance, Dickens tells us in several places[18] in *Little Dorrit* that Dorrit has been broken by his imprisonment, but he shows us that Dorrit was completely incompetent before he came to prison and before Little Dorrit was born. So Dorrit's helplessness, his weeping in Little Dorrit's arms, and his weakness before his death do not seem to us the results of prison. Then too, Dorrit is shown battening on his position in prison[19]—not being broken by it or having been broken by it at all. Perhaps some of the above changes were consciously made by Dickens. Certainly some were probably the result of changes in his ideas. Another inconsistency probably caused by faulty memory is the change in Little Nell in *The Old Curiosity Shop*. She is definitely happy and cheerful until installment 5 when she is suddenly said to be unhappy. Another inconsistency in the same book is seen in Swiveller, who is an unsympathetic character in installments 2, 5, and 14, but a sympathetic character in the rest of the book. Miss La Creevy in *Nicholas Nickleby* goes through a similar change. She is sympathetic in every scene except her first.

Thus we see that Dickens to some extent succumbed to the temptation merely to create advance in plot and that he paid some penalty for this. Undoubtedly there was another side to the coin: Dickens may have been encouraged by this procedure to let his imagination run more freely and to use his mind more spontaneously. At any rate he developed techniques which overcame the worst of this temptation.

SYMBOLIC
ALTERNATION

THE SERIAL'S DEMAND for constant advance in plot did push Dickens and it could have pushed him to the extreme of the authors of those nearly endless stories in *The Arabian Nights* whose plots pile incident on incident and twist upon twist. His criticism of such themeless incident in his remarks about the popular melodrama indicates, however, that he could never willingly submit to such tyranny by the peculiarities of his medium.[1] He worked on this problem from the start and overcame it in several ways. He set up contrasting teams of characters. He developed a kind of loose, alternating pattern of plot, which he made represent patterns he saw in life. He used the irregular plot advance to create impressionistic pictures of some of his more complex subjects. In these two latter ways, then, he forced his form to serve his vision. He came also to use irregular plot advance to arouse curiosity systematically. The representational, impressionistic, and mystifying uses of alternation in plot all tended to relate individual plot advances to a body of central or overall advance. Finally, by means of continuing static symbols and, specifically, symbolic settings used as poles, he managed to weave a plot all of which went in one direction while he pulled first this and then that thread into the fabric. Thus he established both a progression and a polarity despite the obstacles of serial publication.

First, contrasting teams of characters help organize the novels. Since the reader can almost always tell fairly quickly which characters are "good" or "bad," he comes to every new incident with a fund of information (incomplete enough to keep him interested). When he sees a character who is "bad" do something, he knows at once that the action probably will hurt one of the "good" characters, but he does not know how. The individuals tend to be friends or associates of other members of their team, carrying further the organizing tendencies of the division. Thus Carker in *Dombey and Son*, even though he hates Dombey, operates with him to make Edith (and Florence) unhappy. And Toots and Nipper and Walter and Gills and Cuttle try to help Florence. The successes of the "bad" individuals are sensed, then, as successes of the "bad" team or of the opposing forces in life. Similarly the misfortunes of the "good" individuals (Walter's exile, his ship's sinking, Gills's disappearance, Florence's being repulsed by her father, her confusion as her stepmother and her father quarrel) are all felt to be misfortunes occurring to the "good" team—vaguely identified with the main heroine or hero. At its subtlest there is a kind of harmonic and thematic blending of motifs gained from this device, as in *Bleak House*, where the law and people associated with it are involved as antagonists in many incidents.

The alternating pattern of plot is obvious in Dickens's novels, but the thoroughness and the representational use of the alternation may not be. Suppose we follow Martin Chuzzlewit, Jr., and Pecksniff through *Martin Chuzzlewit*. They appear in the following installments and chapters.

Martin		*Pecksniff*	
Installment	Chapter	Installment	Chapter
2	5	1	2, 3
3	6, 7	2	4
5	12	3	6, 8
6	13, 14, 15	4	9, 10
7	16, 17	5	11, 12
9	21, 22, 23	8	18, 19, 20
13	33, 34, 35	10	24
16	43	12	30, 31
18	48, 49, 50	13	35
19	52, 53	16	43, 44
		19	52
10	21	11	19
(out of 19)	(out of 54)	(out of 19)	(out of 54)

Martin Chuzzlewit, Jr., is the closest thing to a main hero the book has. Pecksniff is clearly one of the main villains. Similarly, Esther in *Bleak House* appears in 14 out of 19 installments and in 33 out of 67 chapters.

In the weekly serials the tendency of characters to appear and disappear in successive installments is more pronounced, because there are fewer chapters to each installment. The other serials with lean installments are similar in this respect. This kind of thorough alternation operates as a kind of narrowed and intensified packing with incident and tends in the readers' minds slowly to link the sympathetic characters of all plot threads and also to link the unsympathetic ones.

Thus it helps to convey the organization of the characters into "good" and "bad" teams.

Nell		Quilp	
Installment	Chapter	Installment	Chapter
1	1	3	3, 4
2	2	4	5
3	3	5	6
4	5	7	9
5	6	8	11
7	9	9	13
8	11, 12	13	21
10	15, 16	14	23
11	17, 18	16	27
12	19	20	33
14	24	24	41
15	25, 26	28	48, 49
16	27	29	50, 51
17	28	35	62
18	29, 30	38	67
19	31, 32		
25	42, 43		
26	44, 45		
27	46		
30	52, 53		
31	54, 55		
40	71		
22	32	15	18
(out of 41)	(out of 73)	(out of 41)	(out of 73)

The alternation of plot threads is then underlined by Dickens by his joining of plot materials which are markedly contrasted to each other. *Nicholas Nickleby, The Old Curiosity Shop, Martin Chuzzlewit, Dombey and Son,* and *David Copperfield,* and even *Bleak House, Little Dorrit, Great Expectations,* and *Our Mutual Friend,* are largely devoted to certain domestic events. These involve the rising to fortune of young men or women, unhappy family relations, or love affairs with one reluctant partner—situations within most readers' experience or within limited extensions or projections of such experiences. Yet, in details, many have been intensified until, as in *Dombey and Son,* they are sensational. Unusual and sensational material is also added to each book. In *Nicholas Nickleby,* there are the Yorkshire schools, Ralph Nickleby's exposure of Kate to Hawk, the suicide, and in *The Old Curiosity Shop,* there are Quilp and the framing of Kit. In *Martin Chuzzlewit,* there are Tigg's swindles and his murder. In *Dombey and Son,* there are a host of such events, for example, the shipwreck, Gills's search for Walter, Carker's death, Dombey's bankruptcy. In *David Copperfield,* there are Steerforth's seduction of Emily and Heep's swindling Wickfield. In other books we find similar things: in *Bleak House,* the murder of Tulkinghorn; in *Little Dorrit,* the mystery of the senior Clennams and Rigaud; in *Great Expectations,* Orlick's deeds of violence; and in *Our Mutual Friend,* the deaths of Headstone and Riderhood and of Hexam and the second and third wills of Harmon.

The representational use of the alternation is clear from the evidence. Dickens frankly, though humorously, says that these alternations of plot lines reproduced and represented patterns in life. He says so in *Oliver Twist* as he makes a shift.

It is the custom on the stage: in all good murderous melodramas: to present the tragic and the comic scenes, in as regular alternation, as the layers of red and white in the side of streaky, well-cured bacon. The hero sinks upon his straw bed, weighted down by fetters and misfortunes: and, in the next scene, his faithful but unconscious squire regales the audience with a comic song. We behold, with throbbing bosoms, the heroine in the grasp of a proud and ruthless baron: her virtue and her life alike in danger; drawing forth her dagger to preserve the one at the cost of the other; and just as our expectations are wrought up to the highest pitch, a whistle is heard: and we are straightway transported to the great hall of the castle: where a grey-headed seneschal sings a funny chorus with a funnier body of vassals, who are free of all sorts of places from church vaults to palaces, and roam about in company, carolling perpetually.

Such changes appear absurd; but they are not so unnatural as they would seem at first sight. The transitions in real life from well-spread boards to death-beds, and from mourning weeds to holiday garments, are not a whit less startling; only, there, we are busy actors, instead of passive lookers-on; which makes a vast difference. The actors in the mimic life of the theatre, are blind to violent transitions and abrupt impulses of passion or feeling, which, presented before the eyes of mere spectators, are at once condemned as outrageous and preposterous.

As sudden shiftings of the scene, and rapid changes of time and place, are not only sanctioned in books by long usage, but are by many considered as the great art of authorship: an author's skill in his craft being, by such critics, chiefly estimated with relation to the dilemmas in which he leaves his characters at the end of every chapter: this brief introduction to the present one may perhaps be deemed unnecessary. If so, let it be considered a delicate intimation on the part of the historian that he is going back, directly, to the town in which Oliver Twist was born, the reader taking it for granted that there are good and substantial reasons for making the journey, or he would not be invited to proceed upon such an expedition on any account.[2]

This sermon on the "art" of juxtaposing serious and comic material reminds us of his defense of the Fool in *King Lear*. It also, by the way, is a defense of curtains, and of packing to some extent. In *Nicholas Nickleby*, however, Dickens seems to have associated the abrupt shifting of scenes with unpredictability and romance instead of realism. Again half seriously, he says in *Nicholas Nickleby*, as he comments on a play, that a plot was "delightful . . . as nobody's previous information could afford the remotest glimmering of what would ever come of it."[3]

On the whole, though, Dickens's statements suggest that he seriously believed that this alternation was true to life. Many of his statements suggest the varied, confusing, complex quality of life. Forster mentions his "favourite theory as to the smallness of the world and how things and persons apparently the most unlikely to meet were continually knocking up against each other."[4] Early in his career, commenting on bad news in newspapers, he said: " 'The comfort is, that all the strange and terrible things come uppermost, and that the good and pleasant things are mixed up with every moment of existence so plentifully that we scarcely heed them.' "[5] Forster says, "On the coincidences, resemblances, and surprises of life, Dickens liked especially to dwell . . . people supposed to be far apart were so constantly elbowing each other. . . ."[6]

Dickens's second use of irregular plot advance was to create impressionistic pictures of some complex subjects. The remarks just quoted all suggest that Dickens believed that what seemed unlike or distant was often very similar or close, that contrast and alternation imply vaguely the opposed quantities of unity and continuity. Certainly it is true in a story that the mention of a contrast often suggests the existence of a parallel or a convergence. Dickens appears to have used this fact in his creation of impressionistic pictures built up from contrasts, as well as in his systematic arousing of curiosity and in his use of symbolically polar settings.

His impressionism was based on the fact that each major character had a plot line. When Dickens shifted plot lines, he changed his point of view, for, although Dickens used what might seem at first to be

the omniscient-author point of view, he usually restricted his view to one plot thread at a time. He looked
over the shoulder of one character, often but not always
the most important character, in each subplot, and,
when he changed subplots, he changed observation
posts. In regard to this shifting point of view, Mr.
Boege says: "Few writers . . . have put the first-person method to more varied uses. . . . In dozens of
extended passages he limited his power of omniscience
to a single character, selected for the nonce with almost Jamesian tact. Most sophisticated of all is his deliberate preservation of objectivity."[7] Dickens developed
a technique of showing a character or event from
the several points of view of a number of other characters or spectators. The result is a form of impressionism.[8]

For example, we are shown in installments 13 and
15 in *Bleak House* that Lady Dedlock has cause to fear
Tulkinghorn; we are told in installment 15 that she
leaves her house late at night; we are told in installment 15 that Tulkinghorn is killed; we fear that Lady
Dedlock may be guilty; eventually in installment 17 we
learn that someone else is. Here the impressionism
produces an intense interest in the plot line.

We are shown Chester in installment 6 in *Barnaby
Rudge,* and his politeness and neatness and confidence
make us think him a very pleasant and powerful gentleman. In installment 7 we see him plan with Haredale to break off the engagement of their children by
subterfuge. We note also Chester's overpolite, but contemptuous treatment of Haredale, who appears to be
an honest man, but his enemy. Our opinion of Chester
changes for the worse: we feel that he is slick and
crafty, but we make some allowances for him because
he hates Haredale. And we feel that he is breaking off
the engagement partly because he is an old-fashioned

father and thinks he should be able to command his children. His position seems an honest one, however wrong. In installment 9 we find that Chester is a complete wastrel and wants his son to marry for money in order to restore the family fortune and that he does not really care about his son. In installment 13 we find that the animal Hugh is in Chester's pay and that Chester controls and uses him completely coldly. The picture is now practically complete. Dickens's use of impressionism has let us meet and learn about a character in a lifelike and subtle way. Often Dickens used another method of characterization: he showed and told us what a character was like all at once; but he also used this impressionistic method frequently.

The Gordon Riots, also in *Barnaby Rudge*, Dombey's treatment of his daughter and his second marriage, the French Revolution (in *A Tale of Two Cities*), and the disappearance of Edwin Drood are among the most important subjects of which Dickens attempted to make us feel the depth and several sides by this method.

Dickens's third use of irregular plot advance was to arouse curiosity systematically. His impressionistic technique works because we soon see in a Dickens novel that each character has his own developing plot line and, if we are given several views of one character, we tend to try to fit them together, especially when they conflict at first. In a similar fashion, we try to fit together the plot lines within the one novel and hence tend to try to unify the whole novel. Dickens developed a method for encouraging this unification further by an arrangement of plot arousing constant curiosity and thus pulling his reader from past steps in several plots to the next ones. The arousing of curiosity is carried out by an intensification of the alternation and unit patterns discussed above and by the connection of the story world with some large mystery.

The main tools for this rather elaborate arranging came from the Gothic novel. These devices are used frequently in modern novels of several kinds, and modern commercial novels of the trashiest kind are skillful in this use. So the modern reader tends to feel that the systematic employment of these devices has always been true of fiction and fails to realize that (as far as English fiction is concerned) this group of techniques had once upon a time its own little evolution: a stage of invention, a stage of development, a stage of vigorous exploitation, or some such pattern. And the effects of these techniques may seem somewhat more obvious than they really are and much more familiar to us than to the age of Dickens, when many, many novels were frankly more exposition than presentation. A brief description of aspects of those Gothic novels and of the connections between them and Dickens will help us to analyze his use of these tools. It will also show that he had an important place in the history of their development.

Sir Walter Scott in *The Lives of the Novelists* says Mrs. Radcliffe was the best of the writers of the Gothic novel, which he says is the most popular kind of story.[9] He says that in "chapter after chapter, and incident after incident, [she] maintained the thrilling attraction of awakened curiosity and suspended interest."[10] Scott quotes Mrs. Barbauld, who said Mrs. Radcliffe "seems perfectly to understand that obscurity, as Burke has asserted, is a strong ingredient in the sublime." He expresses a similar view himself and notes her breaking off the narrative when it is "most interesting," her external "contrivance" to make her effects possible.[11] We would say that her novels were full of devices and motifs that made the plots very close to the detective stories of the next century. *The Italian* is typical of her mature style. In it we find a mysterious murder, a strange message, a mysterious building, an investigating hero, a journey to gather clues, arguing from evidence, a court scene with a surprise witness, and foreshadowing. The plot is fast and complex. It involves alternation of story threads, constant interruption, continual defeat of expectation, advancement of the plot in rigidly limited pieces, and virtually regular use of "curtains" or "cliff-hangers."

Mrs. Radcliffe's technique was apparently adopted by Dickens with little change (though, of course, combined with other methods and purposes of his); that is, Dickens added some grand mystery to the story world of a novel and adopted her methods of tightly controlling the alternation of plot threads. Dickens had loved Gothic stories from childhood. The inserted stories in *Pickwick Papers* and the terrifying passages of *Oliver Twist* and *Nicholas Nickleby* show that the taste was strong even at the beginning of his career. The Gothic elements in Dickens's first few books may have been influenced by childhood memories, by the continued, though lessening public interest in Gothic stories, and by contemporary crime novels which used some Gothic elements. Doubtless also they were much influenced by the melodrama of the time. Mr. Chew says of this genre: "Gothic romance influenced the melodramas which were in vogue before a name for them was imported from France" in 1802. "These were spectacular productions, gloomy and mysterious, sometimes introducing the supernatural, infused strongly with sentimental morality, and ending in accordance with 'poetic justice.' "[12] *Oliver Twist* in a general way in Chapter XVII, *Nicholas Nickleby*, passages of other novels, and several of Dickens's articles describe these affairs; there can be little doubt of the influence.

As Dickens wrote magazine serials (*Oliver Twist* and *The Old Curiosity Shop*), he may have turned to magazine serials before his time to see what they could teach him. If he did, he found they were largely

Gothic.[13] By their means or some other he was apparently led to Mrs. Radcliffe.

The Old Curiosity Shop seems to be influenced by a study of Mrs. Radcliffe's work (this connection will be discussed later), but in *Barnaby Rudge* both Mrs. Radcliffe's ideas and techniques begin to be used more thoroughly. The influence of Scott on this novel is well known, but Mrs. Radcliffe's influence is at least as important. The theme, the subject, and the technique of her most finished work, *The Italian,* are reused by Dickens. In *The Italian* she says that villains discuss virtue and that the worldly are wrong to think that this behavior is hypocrisy.[14] She connects it instead to man's pride of reason and sureness that he is right and should force others to be like himself.[15] The behavior of Chester and Mrs. Varden and the mob and Gordon and of many of the characters in Dickens's later books is governed by this principle. Dombey, Murdstone, Gradgrind depend upon it. It is true that this kind of villainy of subjectivity could be developed from Smollett's eccentrics or by reversing Fielding's Parson Adams, but the villains of those men are much simpler. What Mr. Butt and Mrs. Tillotson call the "general moral" of *Barnaby Rudge,* "made explicit in the Preface," is as follows: " 'What we falsely call a religious cry is easily raised by men who have no religion.' "[16] Here and there this theme had appeared mildly in *Pickwick Papers,* but in *Barnaby Rudge* it governs a story of anti-Catholic violence and bigotry. The same theme could be said to govern Mrs. Radcliffe's *Italian,* which is full of Catholic violence and cruelty and zeal, and the closeness of the theme to her remarks about villainy is obvious. In addition *Barnaby Rudge* involves more intense exploitation of curiosity than any of Dickens's previous novels. In the first half of *Barnaby Rudge,* Dickens produced a plot which posed urgent questions for the reader at every move. Mr.

Butt and Mrs. Tillotson say that "he had committed himself to the careful laying-down of clues for the Haredale-Rudge murder-mystery part of the plot."[17]

Barnaby Rudge is also associated with a great many statements about curiosity. A statement Dickens makes in the novel in connection with Gashford's obtaining supporters for Gordon's anti-Catholic movement by skillfully arousing curiosity is interesting. He says: "Curiosity is, and has been from the creation of the world, a master-passion. To awaken it, to gratify it by slight degrees, and yet leave something always in suspense, is to establish the surest hold that can be had, in wrong, on the unthinking portion of mankind."[18] This passage is a virtual paraphrase of Scott's comments on Mrs. Radcliffe; in fact it is a masterful condensation of Scott. In another place in *Barnaby Rudge* Dickens talks of "that appetite for the marvellous and love of the terrible" which have always been in man's nature.[19] Of a minor experience about this time, he remarked, " 'truth is stranger than fiction.' " Evidently the strange and curious were much in his mind at this time. In his next novel, *Martin Chuzzlewit,* he said that all men were secrets,[20] an idea which relates his curiosity to his attempt by humorous and romantic oddity and contrast to make his reader interested in apparently commonplace people and things (compare Hazlitt's idea in *On Imitation* that art should suggest and arouse curiosity).[21]

There are murder mysteries in five of Dickens's fifteen novels. They were used to give a kind of general goal to the slowly advancing and unraveling plots: *Barnaby Rudge, Martin Chuzzlewit, Bleak House, Our Mutual Friend,* and *Edwin Drood.* Furthermore, Dickens was the creator of the first detective in English literature,[22] Inspector Bucket in *Bleak House.* It is interesting to note that when Dickens had developed this technique of suspense in *Barnaby Rudge* in 1841 Wilkie

Collins was only seventeen years old and that in the same year Poe had written *The Murders in the Rue Morgue*. There are lesser mysteries in many other novels as well as in some of the above. In *David Copperfield*, for example, there are mysteries about Uriah Heep, the Strongs, Steerforth, Betsey's husband, etc.

Let us now look at the developed technique of arousing curiosity by careful alternation of plots pointing toward the elimination of these mysteries. Obviously the use of clearly marked stock characters simplifies the reactions of the reader to one of Dickens's serial novels. This fact helped Dickens as he worked. The reader can go over the plot of the Dickens novel with which he is most familiar and note the same phenomena appearing constantly, but I will give here a list from *David Copperfield*, installment 13, of those events which arouse curiosity. We can see what questions are posed by the events.

Chap.		Event		Material Which Causes Event to Arouse Curiosity	Question
38	?	Spenlow confronts David with Miss Murdstone	—	Miss Murdstone has been established as a villainess— therefore is aggressive and therefore is dangerous	(1) What does she intend to do to David?
	—	Spenlow clearly against David as she reveals the love affair	?	Spenlow does not act at once	(2) What will Spenlow do to break up the romance?
	+	David refuses to give Dora up	—	Our knowledge of his vastly improvable financial situation and of his inability to influence Spenlow	(3) What will he do?

(Continued overleaf)

Chap.		Event		Material Which Causes Event to Arouse Curiosity	Question
	+	Spenlow's death	—	Spenlow's being against the affair	(4) What effect will this have on the love affair?
	?	Dora goes to live with Dora's aunts	?	We know nothing at all about them—they are strangers as yet	(5) What will Dora's aunts think about it?
39	—	Heep's display of power	?	Heep does nothing with it at the time	(6) What does he intend to do with this power?
	+	Agnes's promise she will not sacrifice herself	—	We know of no way Agnes can stop Heep—of no person who could help her	(7) What will Agnes do to stop Heep? What will happen to Agnes?
40	?	David sees Martha and Mr. Peggotty	?	We know of no reason why she should be around	(8) What is Martha up to?
	?	Martha listens	?	We know of no reason for her unusually strong interest (though her sympathy and friendship are known)	(9) Why?
	+	Mr. Peggotty has heard of Em'ly	—	Em'ly has run away from home with Steerforth —there has been no news of her	(10) What is Em'ly's state of mind?
	?	Martha disappears		We do not know why, if Martha is so interested, she should not talk to David after Mr. Peggotty goes. We know nothing of Martha's haunts. We know nothing about what she knows.	(11) What is Martha going to do? Where has she gone? What does she know?

In every case the action is advanced so slowly, so gradually, and in such a contradictory way that our curiosity is always aroused. For instance, Question (2) is answered by the same event that poses Question (4). In every case either the event or the material or both are themselves completely unknown (? on chart) to us because Dickens has not revealed enough about them, or a situation favorable (+ on chart) to a sympathetic character has an unfavorable (— on chart) event added to it, or vice versa. The chart can be summed up thus:

$$
\begin{aligned}
\text{Event Number} \quad (1) & \;\; ? \; \& \; - \; = \; ? \\
(2) & \;\; - \; \& \; ? \; = \; ? \\
(3) & \;\; + \; \& \; - \; = \; ? \\
(4) & \;\; + \; \& \; - \; = \; ? \\
(5) & \;\; ? \; \& \; ? \; = \; ? \\
(6) & \;\; - \; \& \; ? \; = \; ? \\
(7) & \;\; + \; \& \; - \; = \; ? \\
(8) & \;\; ? \; \& \; ? \; = \; ? \\
(9) & \;\; ? \; \& \; ? \; = \; ? \\
(10) & \;\; + \; \& \; - \; = \; ? \\
(11) & \;\; ? \; \& \; ? \; = \; ?
\end{aligned}
$$

In other words Dickens always advances at least *part* of his story (for not all the events are being considered) in either a seesaw fashion (+ & —, — & +, and so on) or in steps or pieces which are so small that we do not know which way the plot is going to move until several pieces have been added.

The similarity and connection of both methods to the impressionism mentioned earlier are obvious. The two methods demand a large canvas and great power over arrangement, both of which the serial supplied to Dickens. Once again we see that he turned a potential disadvantage into an advantage as he used his packed and carefully arranged installments to produce the constant (incomplete) satisfaction of curiosity. Moreover, he turned his requirement for constant advances in plot into what are felt as assertions instead of denials of direction because, though adding only a little to the grand picture themselves, his little revelations suggest and bring nearer the grand final illumination of the mysteries (not always, however, at the end of the novel). The curiosity aroused in several plot lines also causes them to blend in motif and mood to some extent, in this way intensifying the fugue quality mentioned earlier. Thus we find Dickens's solutions to his problems blending and reinforcing each other.

Even the symbolic vision of the story world is linked to the controlled alternation of plot lines used to arouse curiosity, for in Dickens there is much symbolic foreshadowing. There are instances of crude foreshadowing: Dickens's statement in *Barnaby Rudge*, after Barnaby and his mother have refused to sell their raven, to the effect that "little did they know what dire future consequences," and so on, is the crudest form possible. Much more important, however, is the frequent use as foreshadowing of symbolically parallel actions or situations of the kind discussed earlier. In *Martin Chuzzlewit* Jonas sees red ink and thinks it is blood—because he is thinking of murdering Tigg. And then Carton's carrying a little girl across a Paris street and asking for a kiss as a reward is an obvious picture in miniature of the last incident in *A Tale of Two Cities*.[24] In *The Old Curiosity Shop* Little Nell's death is foreshadowed by the death of the kind schoolmaster's favorite pupil, and in *A Tale of Two Cities* Darnay's last two unjust trials for his life (and his escapes) are foreshadowed by the trials (and escapes) which have gone before. The most obvious use of this technique in English Gothic fiction is not in Mrs. Radcliffe's works, but in M. G. Lewis's *The Monk*, though I know of no evidence that Dickens read that work. A very effective kind of such foreshadowing is the atmosphere of gloom with which Dickens often hints at the approach of one of the frequent deaths in his novels. Dorrit's driving to Rome through a dark countryside and arriving to find his house darkened except for a small lighted area around his daughter who is sitting by a fire, is one of the most effective examples of this kind. Little Nell's journey through the Black Country is similar. The above examples are, nevertheless, rather trifling examples of this use of parallels. It is also used on a grand scale involving both foreshadowing and enlightened hindsight to clarify and unify whole novels. Thus in *Dombey and Son* Dickens suggests to the reader that Mrs. Brown and her daughter Alice are impoverished counterparts of Mrs. Skewton and her daughter Edith.[25] We later find that Alice's and Edith's fathers were brothers. The oppressors of Alice and Edith were Carker and Dombey respectively (though their behavior was different). The parallel gives considerable significance to Carker's behavior and adds some depth to his character; it also makes clearer and uglier Mrs. Skewton's virtual sale of Edith.

In addition to these three uses of alternating plot for representational, impressionistic, and mystifying purposes, which developed a progression, Dickens set up symbolic poles related to this progression. All the teams of characters and the alternating of plot lines and points of view of course implied polarity. By means of static symbols Dickens expressed the polarity openly. This linking of the symbolic vision of the story world to the controlled alternation of plot lines is much more important than the foreshadowing mentioned earlier. Its methods are interesting. Often in Dickens there are events or situations which hint symbolically at the static character of an important person or group or situation. In *Bleak House* the beautiful, lonely, somehow useless Dedlock estate is a symbol of the character of Lady Dedlock in particular and of the aristocracy in general. Hence it is foreshadowing of a sort because the reader is impelled to draw conclusions about the future behavior of the person and group. But this kind of symbol is really part of the structure of the novel in which it appears. Coketown in *Hard Times*, the prison in *Little Dorrit*, the firm in *Dombey and Son* are other examples of this. Each time such a symbol appears, the unity of the novel is suggested to us as we are reminded of something fundamental to it.

Among the several such symbols in each novel, there are usually two very important ones that are places, and in most cases the novel's plots alternate between them.[26] In other words, most of Dickens's novels are, in a sense, "tales of two cities." Eight of the novels actually develop around two areas, usually towns or cities; five others develop around environments which also form opposing poles. The following table reveals this (in some, a third or fourth area is added).

It is interesting to note that almost always one of these is in the country and the other in London. Usually the country represents a haven, an escape from pain, and London represents a painful or horrible experience. The alternating plot in Dickens, then, is merged with his specific story world, with his personal vision of a world of pain and escape. The alternation of plot lines in its larger patterns becomes associated with his most profound value judgments and his most fundamental symbols. It becomes a slow advance, from a start in pain and orphaning, moving between poles of relief and renewed pain toward a final haven. This pattern is obvious in the main plot lines of *Oliver Twist, The Old Curiosity Shop, David Copperfield,*

Novel	*Poles*
Pickwick Papers	The country, London
Oliver Twist	Rosa's aunt's house, Fagin's
The Old Curiosity Shop	The country, London
Barnaby Rudge	The area near the Maypole (Chigwell), London
Martin Chuzzlewit	The area around Pecksniff's house, London (a third area is America, but this is more or less extra)
Dombey and Son	Gills's, Dombey's
David Copperfield	London, Kent
Bleak House	Bleak House area, London—a third area is the Dedlock household
Hard Times	Stephen's part of Coketown, Bounderby's part of Coketown
Little Dorrit	First half: the Marshalsea, Mrs. Clennam's—Second half: London, Italy (esp. Florence)
A Tale of Two Cities	London, Paris
Great Expectations	Kent, London
Edwin Drood	Cloisterham, London

TOTAL: 13

Great Expectations; it is visible in the parts of *Martin Chuzzlewit, Dombey and Son, Bleak House, Hard Times,* and *Our Mutual Friend.*

We can make sense now of Dickens's more complicated views of his art of plotting. He wrote Forster before finishing the first number of *Dombey and Son,* " 'I think Dombey very strong—with great capacity in its leading idea; plenty of character that is likely to tell; and some rollicking facetiousness, to say nothing of pathos.' "[27] In another letter about that novel, after outlining a carefully narrowed and shaped general plan about Dombey, Dickens adds, " 'So I mean to carry the story on, through all the branches and off-shoots and meanderings that come up.' " Later in that

letter he speaks of Nipper and Toodles and Polly as
" 'what cooks call "the stock of the soup." All kinds of
things will be added to it, of course.' "[28] We note here
his use of a tight plan and offshoots *together*.

Sometimes people suggest that *Great Expectations*
and *Edwin Drood* are somehow departures from this
combination, but Dickens planned *Great Expectations*
as a monthly serial then reluctantly wrote it as a weekly
to help his magazine.[29] Presumably the broader, more
leisurely monthly version would have had expanded,
multiple plots. Then also, his additions of the Orlick
and Wemmick material are incipient extra plots. The
more obvious use of the sprawling complex plot in his
next novel, *Our Mutual Friend,* shows that he was in
no way deserting the cook's mixture.

Edwin Drood may appear to lack "offshoots," but
the impression is misleading, for clearly many plot lines
are merely started when the book breaks off, though
the mystery story seems well developed. Earlier the
plot lines all seemed easily subordinate to the mystery
which developed, but Rosa's story appears to have es-
caped such direct subordination by the time the book
breaks off.[30] Besides, Forster includes in his text a
manuscript he discovered which contains an extra
scene of *Edwin Drood,* detached from the rest of the
story. Forster says: "The scene now discovered might
in this view have been designed to strengthen and carry
forward that element in the tale. . . ." The fragment
is told by Sapsea in the first person. It is humorous and
clever.[31] The fragment and the misgiving mentioned
above are also proof that Dickens to the end of his life
believed in elaborations of a plot with a clear unity as
well.

A passage from the Postscript to *Our Mutual
Friend* sums up Dickens's view of this aspect of his
craft and reveals his suspicion that despite it many

readers remain to some extent in the dark for a long time. " '. . . it would be very unreasonable to expect that many readers, pursuing a story in portions from month to month through nineteen months, will, until they have it before them complete, perceive the relations of its finer threads to the whole pattern which is always before the eyes of the story weaver at his loom. Yet, that I hold the advantages of the mode of publication to outweigh its disadvantages, may be easily believed of one who revived it in the Pickwick Papers after long [*sic*] disuse, and has pursued it ever since.' "[32]

Apparently the poles, as I have called them, are to be seen as fixed quantities in the story world with fixed threads and relationships between them and the alternating plot behaves in some way as the weaver's shuttle, producing before our eyes a varied but unified tapestry.

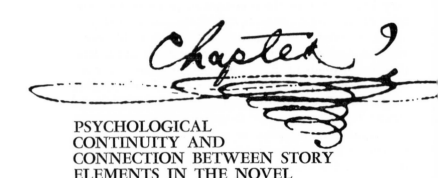

PSYCHOLOGICAL CONTINUITY AND CONNECTION BETWEEN STORY ELEMENTS IN THE NOVEL

THERE IS A PARADOX involved in the picture I have drawn of the novel and the reader's reaction to it. I have asserted that the novel was full of familiar detail and yet insisted that when the reader came to the novel he encountered something new and unknown about which he had to learn and for which he had to find organization of several kinds. Upon reflection, however, we can see that the situation is the same in life. The confusion we feel in unfamiliar but simple situations is never so great as that we feel in familiar and complex situations. In the novel, because of the emphasis upon the individual, we associate ourselves more closely than usual with the characters. Hence here, as in life, we are engulfed by that ignorance which comes from being so close to the trees one cannot see the forest. If there is any ignorance which equals that, it is that of the man who sees only the external material qualities of things but can make no sense out of them because he can perceive or can construct no internal or abstract pattern to them. The ancients, for example, found the behavior of comets and the causes of most diseases to be mysteries and the measurement of variations impossible (without calculus). The ignorance of closeness and the ignorance of externality seize us together whenever we become deeply involved in complicated events. In such situations we attempt to orient ourselves in still another way. We ask, as we also do once immersed in the complexities of a novel, "How does this person with whom I associate myself work or interact with the world about him?" or "How is this incident in which I am involved related to the movements of the world in which it occurs?"

This question about interaction is more complicated and takes longer to answer than "Where am I?" and "What is happening?" The answers found by one kind of person may be very tightly designed and connected. Those found by another may be disconnected, absurd, almost denying that there is good sense in the question yet vaguely responding to its insistence. Still, we are often motivated by some emotion generated by a sense of geography, and encouraged by successful perception of small patterns of event by means of sensitive observation and thought. In such cases most people are likely to attempt to answer "How do we interact with the movement of the world as a whole?" at least in reference to some things. The question involves even more perceptions or assumptions than the simpler ones, for the encompassing world itself is now taken to be moving and changing. The question becomes "Where am I (or are we) within times and spaces in a reality in which the containing time and space may themselves change to others?" In other words, just as "What is happening?" is a refinement of "Where am I?" so "How do I interact with the moving world?" is a refinement of "What is happening?" A more complex question, it requires a more complex mental operation to answer.

Suppose we examine a kind of unfortunate incident and context which occurs frequently and is described again and again in the newspapers, but let us examine it from the point of view of someone involved to such a degree that he tries to prevent a recurrence. Let us take the position of an army major who is asking himself "How are we interacting with the movement of the world here?" because he is shocked to find that when one of his men as a sentry shoots an intruder he is tried for homicide and convicted. Such incidents have happened often to American servicemen since 1945, especially in China, Japan, and the Philippines. Here is what our hypothetical major would find as he investigated. The soldier has been trained to be a sentry and given instructions which he has followed for months: to be alert, to challenge all unrecognized persons, to shoot if they do not identify themselves or if they attempt to attack or to escape. The country in which he is placed on guard over a warehouse is an ally of the United States in the Cold War. The country is embroiled, however, in an internal quarrel about how much if any of the American way of life should be adopted as it tries to become modern. It has many poor; stealing is common among them; and practically all stolen goods can be sold quickly and secretly by them. Thieves succeed in getting past sentries at the post in question or similar posts and succeed in removing American property. The soldier in question hears of these incidents. The American commander protests to local authorities, who are polite, but cannot control the thieves. The Americans erect a high fence with

signs in the local language and add more guard posts—
the soldier in the case is fully aware of these facts—
but ingenious thieves still manage to get through.
Eventually one is killed and later others are wounded
or killed going over the fence. The people of the country, though allies or friends of Americans generally
perhaps, become incensed. They have no love of
thieves, but feel the poor must eat and must do what
they can. They feel that those big, rich Americans can
spare property and need not have shot the thieves.
Their officials protest to the American commanding
general and to Washington, where his superiors warn
him not to let international relations be upset. The
general tells his men to try merely to wound escaping
intruders. The sentries, including the soldier tried
later, become angry at the local population: they feel
that American property is American and stealing is
stealing. One night the soldier in question, a rather
overzealous young man, is surprised suddenly to see a
thief running away and fires quickly. He kills the fugi-
tive, who turns out to be an eleven-year-old boy. The
next day the local people riot and shout "murder." The
local officials demand that the sentry be tried for murder in their courts. They protest to Washington. Trying to pacify the greatest powers involved, and give his
men a warning, the commanding general orders the
sentry tried for homicide in an American court martial.
The sentry is convicted and sent back to the United
States to serve four years in a federal prison.

The major investigating this and hoping somehow
to prevent its happening again is not merely trying to
find out what happened in one incident. He is trying
also to find out how a continuing series of incidents
probably not yet complete is part of a general situation
among enormous masses of people who are themselves
moving in their own directions. He pities the dead

child, but sympathizes more fully with his fellow countryman and fellow soldier, whose states of mind and experiences he shares or can follow. Though space and time are often held to be similar, he will notice that there are vital differences between their operations here. If he can come to any conclusion, he is likely to decide that there is an organic focus in place at the fence near the post where two cultures with very different sets of values confront each other. Here around the clash of individual wills is organized in great waves an international conflict or polarity. If he thinks about the history of the soldier and follows it carefully through time, he is likely to see it in pieces or stages and to decide that there was a moment within time when one of the opposing forces by applying sudden pressure mechanically was able to unravel the opposition and realign it and thus achieve the resolution it wished. If he studies this history further, he will be led to see that there were other points of possible cleavage within time and that one of these was when the sentry attempted to stop the thief. In other words, when the situation is repeated, it is at this point in time, the shooting, that if the major can apply sudden new pressure, he can produce a different, happier resolution. For example, were the next sentry to shoot an air gun loaded with rapidly tranquilizing drug pellets at the thief (as foresters in some places bring bears or other wild animals under control), the thief could be caught with the goods on him and punished more in accordance with his desert. Furthermore, the values of both peoples could be more or less maintained.

In such a situation the observer does not see or envision merely individual facts and a whole geography. Nor does he see merely contrasts and similarities of arrangements of points of fact at different times which form a whole polarity and progression. He sees also great clusters of events (themselves made up of strings and arrangements of points) organized around foci in space. He sees also an inner, abstract continuity, a general movement of the polarized clusters, through time which reveals by contrast cleavages between the individual movements of the parts of each cluster where each can be split. For him history is not merely growth in space. It is instead the intimate process of the clash between two or more growths moving through time and through specific moments in time where one can split, unravel, and realign the other(s).

This kind of vision in regard to abstract matters requires great motivation or preparation; not everybody will trouble himself so long to study, follow, and compare in order to seek the answer to "How do we interact with the moving, changing world?" Yet we use this kind of knowledge everyday. For example, the tennis player does. He throws a tennis ball up in the air with one hand and swings his other arm and drives the ball across the net into an awkward corner of his opponent's court. He does not perceive merely points or planes or strings or arrangements. He sees and uses a whole, shaped interaction of various independent or conflicting facts and operations. Moving within a moving world, he recognizes central, inner, abstract continuities in his opponent, in his own actions, in the movement of the ball, in other quantities such as the mind, in the interaction of all of these. He follows these and their timing so precisely that he can see moments of possible cleavage and resolution and can join and direct the action mechanically when he will. Since history is a matter of mutual pressures and influences, this perception of the continuities and interaction of moving quantities is more important than some academic theory of causation. Up to a point, the more rapid the movement, the more quickly the individual can develop this kind of kinetic perception. The reason for this effect is simple. Stasis encourages a geographic view of life in which unity seems concrete and divisions abstract. Movement encourages a temporal view in which divisions seem clear and unities and continuities seem abstract. Of course we use temporal perception everyday in action: in walking and avoiding collision with other people who are walking; in driving, especially in traffic; in argument; in medical diagnosis; in research; in military campaigns, etc.

In the novel, as was noted above, the reader often asks the question "How do we interact with the changing world?" because he comes to identify himself closely with a character or characters and finds himself immersed in and vicariously participating in a complex of events, pressures, masses of familiar detail in different times and places. In real life the individual tries to answer the question by perceiving beneath the surface of things a focus or foci in space to organizations' conflict and perceiving an abstract continuity, preferably a human one, in the conflict, leading his mind eventually to a point within time when cleavage, redirection, and resolution of tension are possible. The novelist employs this fact. Within his subject he seeks a pattern of focus in space, continuity, cleavage within time and presents the reader with such a pattern to help him organize the masses of familiar detail and see what the author regards as the meaning of his novel. Since the novelist is dealing with individuals, the focus, continuity, and cleavage are individual and psychological. A great deal of the individual's life consists of internal feelings, though there is also a large amount of external action in individual life, action directed by both internal feeling and external forces. The consequence is that, especially in the work of a novelist like Dickens with a view of normal man as passive, a great deal of this focus, continuity, and cleavage is presented in novels by pictures of psychological states.

A public work like the *Iliad* or *Prometheus Bound* assumes that character or consciousness is a single thing; such works do not devote much space to psychological states. The private fact of individual life, however, is very different; so individualistic forms of art are different. A man gets up in the morning and finds himself in a certain mood. After shaving he may feel wholly different; after breakfast, he may be in a state different from his former two; and so on through the day. Then some men are in one world of responsibilities and comforts or of noise and oppression with their families, in another of rapid decision and activity or anxieties or mere marking time with their jobs, in still another all alone with dreams of success or worries about little aches and pains, etc., etc. In both place and time, an individual may be many people, sometimes two or more at once (as when daydreaming while dialing to make a business phone call from his home). In such circumstances, then, the individual's personal form of the question "How do I interact with the changing world?" may easily boil down to "Who am I?" In the novel, it becomes "Who is this person with whom I identify myself?" and the focus, continuity, and cleavage are aids to finding the answer, to making sense of the many details of psychological states which are presented, to relating the different states or aspects of single psyches.

It is also true that public actions very often have obvious public explanations, whether verifiable ones or not. A person may say "Hitler invaded Poland because he wanted to rule the world." Private actions often have no such obvious public explanation and need an explanation related to private feelings and states of mind. Much of the external, public, social life of man is carefully and formally organized. As we have noted, no such obvious clarity is found within an individual psyche. To suggest the meaning of private actions by private feelings would be little help to the reader then, unless the private, inner life of a character was shown to have some pattern. Showing such pattern for many individuals is awkward; so most novels concentrate on one major character and two or three lesser ones. In practice, the establishment of focus, continuity, and cleavage is usually to give a sense of design within one character and related design between that character and other people and things, between him and his world, in short.

The use of a focus in place, an inner continuity, and a cleavage within time can be seen easily in the novel *Jane Eyre*. The focus of the novel is a struggle. On one side are Jane's drives to be herself in peace and to receive love from others. On the other side is a society made up of Mrs. Reed, school, Rochester, and St. John, which is by turns hostile and dangerous, vaguely permissive, and willing to give love if she gives up self or to accept self if she gives up love. Jane seems to recognize from the start that to be oneself in peace and to receive love from others are conditions which require each other. The society storms and stamps, and bribes, and tempts. Jane is truthful and industrious and insistent. They talk and argue back and forth. The society slowly yields, collapses, and is realigned at the end with Jane as heiress, beloved wife, and nurse-mother.

The focus obviously overlaps with what I have called the polarity of the novel, yet includes the conditions and materials of the struggle as well as the strugglers. There is a progression from Mrs. Reed's house to Lowood, from pupil to teacher, from Lowood to Rochester's household, from governess of the child to sweetheart of the master, from Thornfield to Moor House (her cousins'), and back to Thornfield. It is accompanied by Jane's gaining acceptance and respect at the school, love at Thornfield, admiration at Moor House, virtually imperial or divine stature at the end. (For a discussion of this absolute power of hers and some consequences, see G. A. Graig's brilliant article "The Unpoetic Compromise," in *Society and Self in the Novel*, ed. Mark Schorer [New York, 1955]). There is, however, no connection between the parts of the society which make these various concessions to Jane, and, regarded from the outside, the progression would be clear but the causes of individual events would not.

Yet there is an internal continuity and truth, and many readers are led to feel Jane and her fortune are right. We follow the feelings of Jane: her outrage at the injustice of Mrs. Reed, her difficulties at school, her romantic and sympathetic reactions to Rochester, etc. Seen from this angle there are within the story time repeated points where Jane can sally forth, split her opponent, and gain an advantage. She repeatedly beats Mrs. Reed in argument and eventually silences her. She can show how Helen's ideology is too simple for her, Jane. She can show Rochester how her being his mistress would take away her stature, value, and self. And so on. She can overcome Mrs. Reed, because Mrs. Reed is unfair, but believes in consistency and because there are other people in the world (Jane makes much of the presence in the house of Mr. Lloyd the apothecary). She can overcome Rochester because he has been shown to have done something wrong (persuading her to marry him, although he is already married). Again and again the opposing society pushes too far and becomes off balance. Then Jane, ever alert, pushes it in the direction she wants. The ending is inevitable, for she is willing to wait and hammer away to whatever extent life requires. She is young and likely to survive the mad, older wife. Once Jane has gone, Rochester is sure to see that he needs Jane's love as much as she needs his. Rochester is calamity-prone (he was trapped into marriage, fell from his horse, nearly got burned, etc.) and is bound for a ruin in which she can become ruler. In this novel, as in life, the individual by following his feelings and delicate responses to the outside world can locate the points within time where splitting, or cleaving, and unraveling and realigning the opposed force are possible. This novel is not unusual in having more than one such point, though many emphasize only a final one.

Although this kind of orientation is used in life and in fiction, modern relativity theory appears at first to deny its possibility. Since time and space values depend on one's frame of reference in a moving universe, it is hard to show that two events occur in different places at the same time. Much of the trouble perhaps comes from discussing time as only one dimension added to length, width, and height. This system does not explain how a football player can ever catch a forward pass except by accident, and the lovers whose two hearts beat as one are not allowed, and the barbershop quartet has never been.

The whole picture sounds familiar, because it is really an adaptation of some of Kant's view to physics. Moreover, the theory is applied to abstract and specialized subjects extremely hard to assess (atoms, stars, light, etc.).

It might be more consistent with the general idea of a space-time continuum to consider time as perhaps as complex as space. It would also be more consistent with the general idea of related motion to worry less about measuring things in themselves and to observe things in related clusters. Then forward passes, the sympathies of lovers, barbershop quartets, etc., would make more sense. In the world of every day, we can see that time and space are locked in such complex relationships, which we can describe. Not only is it not impossible to demonstrate that two things happen in different places at the same time, much of life requires synchronized movement and can be explained only in terms of it. Let us consider two dancers. As they turn and step, they move in different directions. They are in different places. Yet we can see and hear that they are in time with each other and with the orchestra. Their dance is not the momentary intersection of two lines, but the graceful, long-continued movement of two beings in constant contact and co-operation. Two tennis players follow similar patterns during a match. We can see that each is locked, abstractly of course, into a relationship to the other player's movements and the tennis ball's movements, in order to play the game at all. The partnership here is partly antagonistic, but it is still a co-operation. Perhaps two dancers and two tennis players would not be regarded as operating in different places. We can extend the picture. A man on a mountain can see bombs dropping from planes and simultaneously the citizens of a town running for cover far below. An astronaut in a satellite whirling around the earth can see at the same instant a storm drifting over one state and a flood already started by it going on in another. In short, frames of reference from which simultaneous actions can be observed can be set up and can have a special usefulness to human beings. Much of life consists of such pairs of things which co-operate continuously often for prolonged periods in contact with each other. Such are the relations of one person to his employer or of a people to the raw materials of its country or of an artist to his painting, and hundreds of other common activities. It is the frequency of such patterns which causes us, despite theories about some special subjects, despite clichés about subjectivity and alienation, and despite claims of universal absurdity, to seek in life and in novels the complex orientation of a focus in place, an inner continuity, and a point of cleavage within time.

For Dickens the focus in place, psychological continuity, and point of cleavage within time took a particular form. The next chapter will show that the serial's constant breaks and its encouragement of shifts made the relation of character to events and of events to events unusually difficult. Critics attacked him for this, and since the portrayal of a *steadily* developing process or the analysis of anything was so difficult, Dickens was sometimes content with a superficial picture of a fashionable social abuse, with a sort of costume drama of poverty or misfortune. The serial's length and shifts, which were exaggerations of what one would find in any novel, intensified the reader's need of some inner relation between the selves of the protagonist and between those selves and his world. Dickens was tempted to use Fielding's old trick (from Greek tragedy and romance originally) of having everybody turn out to be related to everybody in the end. This amounted to an allegorical statement of connection, though readers hardly felt it to be the fact of relationship embodied and made palpable. Like many symbolic and allegorical statements, it often omitted explanation or illustration of believable processes in familiar contexts and was ineffectual art.

Yet Dickens was a great novelist and, as the chapter after next shows, his unified vision of life led him to try again and again to improve this aspect of his art, which underwent great change during his artistic career. The continuity in the novel, as I have suggested, is fundamentally internal and personal. The novel may at its best have external continuity, or absence of same by design, for that is a relationship, too. But it can make do without it, as we saw *Jane Eyre* did. Serialization made the kind of simple external continuity we find in *Henry V* or Aeschylus' *Libation-Bearers* most unusually difficult for Dickens. So when he felt a need for continuity, he was forced to develop the inner, psychological kind. Furthermore, since his external materials were especially scattered and separated and the steady development of any process required extraordinary effort, it is not strange to find that he took one step after another to improve this psychological continuity. The matter was magnified so much by the serial that it was clear it really amounted to the arrangement within spaces and times of pictures of psychological states or the external facts associated with them. This was the easier to see because Dickens believed man was passive and often saw the world as simple stimulus. His mere arrangements of events within space and time became, with some adjustment, arrangements within psyches quite naturally. The matters of foci and points of cleavage were solved for Dickens by his peculiar philosophy. The focus of a Dickensian story was usually a struggle of a villain or an environment with a passive protagonist. The points of cleavage are least well handled and are usually moods of decency or weakness which overcome villains and soften them or the presence in evil environments of mysterious, strong, active rescuers. The former of these was capable of realistic development and eventually received it.

Dickens's use of focus in space, continuity, cleavage within time developed in a five-fold pattern. He started by creating story from character. He related his characters and situations by using a passive protagonist tied to a villain or oppressive environment. He probed and analyzed character more often. He came to use a biographical story pattern and point of view. Finally, he deepened his treatment of the reform plot. In short, he came to see his story as the reform of a maturing passive protagonist and was able to fuse his symbolic world and his alternating, mystery plot with the self-discovery of the chief character.

Chapter 10

SERIAL INTERRUPTION OF PROCESS

THE GRAVEST PROBLEM presented to Dickens in intermittent publication was the extremely difficult task of establishing organic connections between characters, situations, and events. Symbolic and allegorical unity achieved by parallels and poles did not suffice in this matter. Specifically, it involved making his audience feel that there was an inner sense to his story; that a given character was behaving as he would in the same situation in life; that from this behavior an appropriate event would develop similar in its shape and timing to its counterpart in life; that this event would perhaps lead to another appropriate event and then another reaction or action by the character, etc., in a way similar to a line of development in history. Since a process is usually felt to move *steadily*, a story that is full of gaps between installments, shifts in scene, etc., makes a convincing imitation of real processes hard to produce. The critics of Dickens's own day became aware of this problem and grew dissatisfied with the serial.[1] Indeed, the lack of organic unity was one of the aspects of Dickens's work most often attacked, according to Ford.[2]

As did the problems of spatial and temporal arrangement, the problem of presenting process gave Dickens most difficulty in the early years of his career, but gradually, and with occasional lapses, Dickens worked his way beyond the disconnectedness and lack of involvement in his subject matter into which this serial problem pushed him. I shall discuss the problem in this chapter and and Dickens's solution later. The oddities in the stories Dickens produced before he solved the problem can help us understand his eventual solution.

The serial's demand for many incidents and its constant interruptions encouraged Dickens's use of certain kinds of incident which do not require or permit the connection of character and event, or event and event. Some of these doubtless seemed appropriate to his casual, rather disconnected view of life.

The main kinds of such incidents are coincidences and calamities and crimes. Magnus just happens to be a very jealous man and happens to be the future husband of the lady into whose room Pickwick gets by mistake—hence the arrest of the club members and the exposure of Jingle to the Nupkins family. Oliver Twist just happens to be sent off on an errand as Nancy and Sikes are passing and is thus recaptured. Cheeryble just happens to be looking in the employment office window when Nicholas Nickleby is—hence his rescue of the Nickleby family. The reader can add to the list of coincidences indefinitely. Jaggers just happens to be Miss Havisham's lawyer as well as Provis's. Carton just happens to be Darnay's double. And so on.

The calamities are also numerous. Someone in almost every book falls sick and his sickness affects the plot for a little way. Rose Maylie's sickness causes Oliver Twist to bump into Monks and causes Harry to propose. Little Nell's sickness in *The Old Curiosity Shop* causes her death. Martin Chuzzlewit's sickness helps cause his change in character. Esther's sickness in *Bleak House* causes Guppy to withdraw his proposal and makes less important Lady Dedlock's disclosure that she is Esther's mother. And so on. There are several deaths in every book. There are several murders and several swindles and innumerable minor villainies (Smallweed's threatening to ruin George and his friend Bagnet in *Bleak House*, Mrs. Clennam's suppression of a codicil to her husband's uncle's will in *Little Dorrit*, Miss Havisham's pretense that she is Pip's benefactor in *Great Expectations*, and so on).

Now to argue that these events have no connections at all with other events would be absurd. But connecting events is very difficult when so many of them are sensational. Generally, few causes or results are shown in the early novels. A coincidence or a calamity has no connection usually with the characters of the people involved, anyway, and a crime or villainy has frequently little connection with the character of the victim. Furthermore, Dickens tends to hide the development of a situation which precedes an event rather than to dwell upon it and study it openly. As we saw earlier, he emphasizes surprise.

The result of the use of coincidences, calamities, crimes, and villainies, often practically to the exclusion of other events, is that the characters of the protagonists have almost nothing to do with the stories in some of Dickens's novels except to regulate the poetic justice, symbolic of the divine, in the endings. Their fortunes go up or go down because of events outside their control, that is, because of the actions of environment or of villains or of benefactors. In addition, the plots tend to become mere loose bundles of unrelated coincidences, calamities, and so on.

Thus *Oliver Twist* is a tissue of coincidences (in

this book Dickens calls them "fate"):[3] Brownlow happens to pity Oliver and happens to be his father's best friend. Fagin happens to be in Monk's employ. Oliver happens to be hurt robbing a household which pities him and which happens to contain his aunt (Rose). And so on. Each coincidence is enough to produce a little bit more of the plot or of the situation which is unfolded but never enough to produce all the rest, for Dickens does not develop any of the situations produced. Brownlow happens to pity Oliver and happens to be his father's best friend, but, after he has taken Oliver in and has noticed the amazing similarity between Oliver and the picture of his friend's lover, he does nothing for a long time which the story focuses on. No, another coincidence occurs. Nancy and Sikes happen to meet Oliver—by chance, not because they have been searching London systematically. Oliver is taken back to Fagin. Dickens does not develop Oliver's situation there very far, before another coincidence, Oliver's getting shot on his first robbery, whisks Oliver off to safety. Now there is no relation between Brownlow's taking in Oliver and Oliver's being shot, nor between Nancy's recapture of Oliver and Oliver's being shot. Thus these coincidences make the continuation of the story possible, but do not relate its parts to one another. They make it possible for Dickens to use a character already familiar to the reader because of previous installments in an almost totally new situation without having any troublesome worries about whether the character's traits or those of other characters would ever naturally cause him to land in the new situation.

Calamities tend to operate in the same way coincidences do. In *The Old Curiosity Shop* Nell's grandfather (a) loses all he has, (b) falls sick, (c) becomes senile. Later Nell finds out (d) that he gambles, then

(e) that he plans to steal. They go without food for several days (f). Nell (g) sickens and (h) dies. (a) is not directly related to (h), for a series of other calamities is necessary to go from (a) to (h). (a), (b), and (c) are perhaps related. So perhaps are (d) and (e) on one hand and (f), (g), and (h) on the other. But the various sets are not related to one another. It takes eight calamities to get Nell dead. No one of the situations is developed very much; instead, Dickens adds new calamities, thus destroying all possible connection between one set of events and the next.

Crime and villainy often operate in much the same way, for many of Dickens's villains are not villains in any particular way. Thus Pecksniff, the hypocrite in *Martin Chuzzlewit,* does nothing else so villainous as his telling Mary Graham she had better marry him or he will hurt her lover, Martin Chuzzlewit, Jr., by making Martin's grandfather angry at him. Yet this threat is not a hypocritical act. Pecksniff fires Pinch after telling Martin Chuzzlewit, Sr., lies about him; this is not hypocrisy. Pecksniff steals Martin Chuzzlewit, Jr.'s, design for a school. This is not hypocrisy. Pecksniff is a hypocrite, but his *main* villainies are not connected with his character, though the acts are made to seem more credible by being made the acts of a single person. But none of his evil deeds is related to any of the others. There are exceptions to this rule about Dickens's villains, especially among the noncriminal antagonists. Smallweed and Miss Havisham, for instance, act mainly in character. In general, however, the mean and villainous acts are done in isolation or are connected only by an old rule of psychology. That old rule says that all evil comes from pride, all virtue from love, and that therefore the doer of one evil act will do any other. Thus Pecksniff threatens Mary; then, when Mary tells Pinch, he slanders Pinch and

fires him. Many other characters exhibit the same dis-
connection between their personalities and deeds and
fortunes: Nicholas Nickleby, Dombey, Lady Dedlock,
Carton, for example.

Not only did the serial interruptions make difficult
the organic development of plot from situation, event,
or character by encouraging the use of individual subjects and events that had little to do with each other.
But, also, serial interruptions worked directly, and
simply broke up relations or caused people not to see
relations that the author established, as Dickens's postscript to *Our Mutual Friend* suggested (see the end of
Chapter 8). One part of the plot did not easily build on
another, and the parts did not build easily on a basic
personal relationship or on the characters. The situation doubtless discouraged Dickens at first. Such a
building procedure always requires the author to think
and care about his subject a good deal, and the serial
interruptions must have made the effort seem almost
pointless at times.

What might have happened to the plot of one of
Dickens's early stories if he had thought about it is instructive. Let us suppose that Dickens had taken the
one interesting psychological situation in *The Old
Curiosity Shop*, Trent's gambling, and analyzed it. The
story might have started at Trent's decision to gamble,
shown the terrible effects of gambling on him and Nell,
led to a crime on his part to get money to gamble with
(much like what almost happens at one point in *The
Old Curiosity Shop*), ended in his capture, punishment,
and death—after he had seen how he had ruined himself and hurt Nell. The main character of such a story
would be Trent, not Nell. But the story would be as
sensational as the historical one.

What Dickens actually did resembles in parts
what I have outlined, but other people's stories (Quilp's

and Kit's among others) interrupt and complicate the tale. Then Dickens did not use the decision, the crime, the realization of the blame mentioned above. Instead he showed the effects of gambling: the loss of the shop early in the book, and then, after a long interval, the planned robbery among other things later in the book. This gambling and other sensational events, such as wandering as beggars and going without food, end in Nell's death, which is, however, not a result of a chain of causes and effects. Dickens battered the girl with separate calamities. The parts of the book are devoted to the separate calamities, not to parts of one. The best situation in the book is not developed except sporadically and incompletely and out of focus (with Nell as the center of interest). Irrelevant material instead of being eliminated is dragged in by the cartload. The real problem of Trent is confused and disintegrated by the addition of other sensations.

Perhaps passive protagonists suggested at first that no solution of story problems could occur and hence that no thought about, or involvement in them, was worthwhile. Dickens was very interested in such social problems as the hardships of the poor, unhappy marriage, oppression by relatives, fanaticism, bad government, and crime. He introduced these into his stories constantly. Yet he rarely analyzed them (in his fiction). Perhaps he felt such analyses would be too difficult; he objected to such a work by Mrs. Gaskell (see the last note in Chapter 4). Dickens's readers are usually given pictures of poverty or marital unhappiness only, not glimpses of what makes women shrews or what makes a fanatic or what creates the Circumlocution Office. Disagreeable people in many of Dickens's books are outwitted or crushed or left victorious in ways commoner to fiction than relevant to life. The piling of misfortune and abuse on the unpleasant

Miggs at the end of *Barnaby Rudge* is an example. His novels are full of people who are unable to save money or earn it or who are eager to amass it or who receive it gladly when they are given it. In short, Dickens has a sort of preoccupation with money. But he calls businessmen villains and schemers.[4] He almost never shows or describes them at work; when he does, they are shown being crooked or at least harsh. One wonders if he remembered what most businessmen did in their offices when they worked. It seems fairly clear that he did not analyze the problems of the businessman or those created by him—never analyzed the problems of creating, distributing, or getting wealth. He fills his books with "born" villains or heroes. He does not show the environment acting on Oliver Twist and Oliver Twist reacting to it and rejecting it; he has Fagin say simply that Oliver is better than other boys.[5]

Dickens seems mainly interested in such social materials as suppliers of personal incidents. One extraordinary proof of this statement is the fact that Dickens constantly attacked debtors' prison, pocket boroughs, and other evils which had been eliminated or greatly lessened by the time Dickens wrote his books and often set the events in his books in an era before he himself was adult.[6]

Dickens's frequent procedure with regard to social problems is demonstrated by Mr. Butt and Mrs. Tillotson's extraordinary account of the topicality and closely followed sources of *Bleak House*.[7] This novel is unusually topical even for Dickens, but what is important is that the borrowed ideas in the novel skimmed its social subjects, however skillful their presentation. *Hard Times* gets even less close to its social subjects. Only in the middle of the book does Dickens deal with "industrial unrest." "But he made little attempt to discuss the problems" involved. "In fact he scarcely went beyond the comments of *The Times* reporter." The "industrial theme" is then dropped until the scene near the end of the novel where Stephen is found.[8]

Dickens might have continued to use his belief that life was rather disconnected as an excuse for stories which were even more broken up than some aspects of experience. He might have continued paradoxically to be passionately involved in certain subjects and still merely skim them in his novels. The historical fact is, however, that he overcame these problems, too. Never deserting his view of life, he found ways of relating its parts so that they seemed more widely acceptable, and he developed means of probing abstract and social subjects in fiction and of expressing more of his concern in his works.

Chapter 11

IDENTIFICATION
WITH A MATURING
PASSIVE PROTAGONIST

THE SERIAL INTERRUPTIONS which drive an author toward disconnectedness and a lack of involvement in subject might have reduced a less serious man than Dickens to a facile, insincere entertainer, but Dickens, as a great deal of evidence shows, was deeply involved in his characters and was tremendously in earnest about the social problems of his day.[1] In time this earnestness helped him solve his most serious problem with the serial story.

Essentially his techniques for arranging materials in space and time, most of which he developed in the first third of his career, assumed a passive reader who had stimuli presented to him by an active author. When the author himself had no particular reaction or other personal relationship to these stimuli, the result was a rather shallow impression on the reader no matter how artful the arrangement or how intellectually extensive the allegory. Dickens's earnestness, however, seems to have caused him to relate himself personally more and more to these stimuli as he matured as an artist. Despite his aggressiveness in his career, his private view of the relation of his self to his world seems to have been a picture of a passive reaction. His sympathies and his philosophy both led him to associate himself with social victims and those who were passively influenced. Perhaps, as a result, he more and more associated himself with the passive reader. Accompanying this association came a tendency to create plots around protagonists who were closer and closer to this passive self and passive reader—protagonists with whom both Dickens and the reader could become increasingly identified.

This change came about in four steps, each marked by Dickens's adoption of a certain method of writing or device: the creation of anxiety about the protagonist, the analysis of a situation or event while looking over the shoulder of one character, the fully biographical approach, the focusing upon a psychological reformation resulting from certain experiences. Each device came to be used systematically by Dickens with the writing of a specific novel. Let us trace this history briefly.

Perhaps I should explain what I mean by a "passive protagonist." I mean primarily a protagonist who does not plan and does not direct events or arrange the stage props of his world, one whose main behavior is reacting, although he may work in some routine fashion or may move about physically. Pickwick and Nicholas Nickleby seem to me athletic and aggressive. Oliver Twist and Little Nell are pursued by others, but still athletic and still capable of taking the initiative. The protagonists and many of the antagonists of later novels, however, are strikingly limp or sedentary, at least psychologically, and are more reflectively sensi-

tive. Perhaps we could say that the aggressive picaresque protagonist inherited from Smollett did not fit
the passive view of character which Dickens acquired
from the sensibility tradition; that Dickens modified the
picaro and developed a whole method of storytelling
which suited the passive kind of protagonist he chose.
Thus Dickens's progress as an artist involved a continual increasing of the role of the passive protagonist
in the novel until Dickens was able to see his arrangements in space and time as the stimuli presented to a
character reaching inner maturity and was thus able
to fuse his artful arrangement, his alternating progress, and an organic plot convincingly imitating a
mental process observable in real life.

a) the point of departure

The development in Dickens's art outlined above
was made possible by a procedure Dickens used
throughout his career. Dickens created story from
character. We need to examine this habit as a point of
departure before we trace the changes in his art.
Romantic criticism of Shakespeare in Germany and
England had emphasized character more than plot
structure. Much of Smollett, as Mr. Kahrl's book[2]
shows, was built from character, comparison of character, and conflict of character with itself, with others,
with surroundings. Fielding had talked of himself as
a biographer occasionally in *Tom Jones*. Many eight-
eenth- and nineteenth-century novelists had done the
same, including Defoe in *Moll Flanders* and the crime
novelists of the 1830's. In fact, the whole empirical
drift of much of English thought and art made the procedure from character to plot a natural one for Dickens.

Forster's quotations of letters from Dickens show
him always worrying about names and hence presum-

ably characters (and other things by names as a short-hand) when he was forming a plot in his mind before he wrote a novel.[3] An examination of the novels reveals some organization, perhaps unconscious, by means of associations of names. With the name Oliver, which suggests Cromwell to an Englishman, he associated the idea of decapitation (as of King Charles I) and the name Monks (the name of a general under the Cromwells) in *Oliver Twist*. In *David Copperfield* he associated the name David, Agnes (from lamb of God), Uriah, a man called Ham with a "betrayed" sister, a rebellious son, the notion of more than one wife, the idea of sexual trickery. All of these things can be found in the story of David in the Books of Samuel. In *Bleak House* an Esther almost marries and does rescue in a way parallel to the Biblical Esther. In *Little Dorrit* a pallid Tennysonian Arthur loses a woman he loves and weakly, though idealistically, tries to patch up a world he cannot control. In *A Tale of Two Cities* a Charles almost loses his head and a Sidney like Sir Philip is a perfect knight and gentleman and loses the girl he loves. In short, when his main characters had famous names, the events associated with them were vaguely parallel to those associated with those names in history or in famous story. His needing to know the names of his main characters before he could begin a novel, then, meant he had to know some of the main emotional situation or plot at least unconsciously before he could feel confident. Lindsay has shown that some of the other names in Dickens have autobiographical significances. Whether Dickens was aware of all of these is questionable. We must presume that all his names had strong associations for him. Forster shows he collected odd names (see note 3), presumably as ammunition so to speak.

The process of construction from characters is in-

disputable. Dickens talks in a letter during the composition of *Barnaby Rudge* of having been able to " 'build
greatly on the Varden household.' "[4] Forster talks of
Martin Chuzzlewit's "origin" being in "the notion of
taking Pecksniff for a type of character . . . the design
being to show, more or less by every person introduced,
the number and variety of humours and vices that have
their root in selfishness."[5] *Dombey and Son* was at
first supposed to work the same way with pride.[6] In
other words one character could lead to a cluster and
through incident to an illustration of a theme. In a
letter about *Dombey and Son* Dickens says that Toodles
and Polly and Nipper are " 'the stock of the soup' " to
which many " 'things will be added' "[7] later.

Another letter about *Dombey and Son* expresses
hope because the first installment has "plenty of character that is likely to tell."[8] It is obvious that in the first
halves of his books, where he was building, he poured
in dozens of new characters. Forster says of *Edwin
Drood* that Dickens feared "that he might have plunged
too soon into the incidents leading on to the catastrophe" and so decided "to open some fresh veins of character" connected with the plot but "not directly part of
it" and to build them around Sapsea, delaying but
emphasizing the end of the story.[9] So Dickens was conscious of this part of his technique. His novels devote
a great deal of space to the description of characters
and the presentation of characteristic dialogue and
minor action. Clearly, then, much in his books that is
not strictly narrative progression also develops from
character.

There was an unpredictable element in this conduct of the story. Dickens speaks in an announcement
to his readers after *Barnaby Rudge* of "the gradual development of my characters" during his serial novels.[10]
Any reader can see the way new sides are added to

some characters like Mrs. Gamp as the novels continue. A letter during the composition of *Martin Chuzzlewit* shows where this process led Dickens: " 'as to the way in which these characters have opened out, that is to me one of the most surprising processes of the mind in this sort of invention. Given what one knows, what one does not know springs up.' " Forster adds, "The remark displays exactly what in *all* his important characters [my italics] was the very process of creation with him."[11]

Clearly, for a man who identified himself so closely with his characters and felt they were real, such a process must lead to the plot's often escaping his conscious control. Dickens said, " '[Fagin is] such an out and outer that I don't know what to make of him [at the end of the novel].' " Forster's comment is "No small difficulty to an inventor, where the creatures of his invention are found to be as real as himself." Forster also says of *Oliver Twist* that "the story *shaped itself* to its close [my italics]."[12] Later Forster compares Dickens's sketch of his plan for one of the Christmas books, *The Chimes* (these were published as wholes only) with the final story. He says that "comparison with tale as printed" lets us "see the strength of *its* mastery over his first design [my italics]," and gives "a good illustration of his method in *all* his writing [my italics]." "Thus always, whether his tale was to be written in one or in twenty numbers, his fancies controlled him. He never, in any of his books, accomplished what he had wholly preconceived, often as he attempted it. Few men of genius ever did . . . . where characters are so real as to be treated as existences, their creator himself cannot help them having their own wills and ways."[13] Yet we should note that a "first design" or a preconception is said to have existed.

Dickens's belief in a prophetic quality in art led

then at times to a kind of spontaneous composition. Dickens announced in a letter about *The Chimes* " '[the story] has great possession of me every moment in the day; and drags me where it will.' "[14] Now extravagant comic analogies were admitted by Dickens to be characteristic of his mind.[15] Starting with character Dickens could proceed to incident, to analogous characters and incidents, to distortions and fantastic situations. Finally he could develop a story until he reached the realistic elaboration and the elaborate parallels and contrasts of Dora and Agnes, Ham and Steerforth, etc., which Mr. Butt and Mrs. Tillotson show exist in the notes and plans of *David Copperfield* as well as the finished book.[16]

This method of composition built upon characters as absolutes, which in a sense they were to Dickens, since he believed in their reality and felt very intensely about them, often in sympathy with them. The partial unpredictability of this method of the creation of plot diminished as Dickens matured. His ability to develop parts of his stories organically increased as he extended this base in which he believed and about which he cared.

b) the creation of anxiety about the protagonist

The first step in Dickens's development of the role of the passive protagonist was apparently another result of the influence of Mrs. Radcliffe. From her Dickens learned about a kind of story in which the protagonist was persecuted in a series of sensational incidents.

Let us look briefly at this terrifying aspect of the Gothic novel, in which Scott had said Mrs. Radcliffe's works were the best. Scott compares the Gothic novel to the melodrama in that it too is aimed at the creation of "fear." "The force" of it "lies in the delineation of external incident." The people are mere types. "It does not appeal to the judgment . . . or stir the passions."[17] As to Mrs. Radcliffe, "The public were chiefly aroused . . . by the wonderful conduct of a story, in which the author so successfully called out the feelings of mystery and of awe . . ."[18] She employed heroines constantly in danger.[19] In short, she was a master at arousing perpetual anxiety.

Mrs. Radcliffe undoubtedly learned much about suspense from Richardson and his followers. They had written about the heroine of delicate sentiments in a more or less fixed general situation of peril because of the varied and sensational actions of a villain. They had mastered the careful, even mechanical, control of proportions within books (a natural development in a work like *Familiar Letters*). They had used the raising of questions left unanswered and the switching of subjects and the linking of separate incidents (natural in letters). They had developed the externally manipulated plot (natural enough in a letter book), which moves in unpredictable manner but at a steady, mathematically regulated pace toward an obvious end. They had delighted in the curious emphasis on the rather common heroine's observations of, and minor reactions to, a kind of pageant of danger which moves before her eyes without causing any deep permanent change within her. And they too had been charmed by the Cinderella motif.

Yet in Mrs. Radcliffe's own novels these devices were developed and intensified. The villain was made both more criminal and more sensitive. The heroine and hero became more passive; the number of events and plots and the pace of the story were greatly increased. The space allowed to the normal and predictable heroine's reactions was cut down. The device of letters was dropped. The number of coincidences was greatly increased. In the place of Richardson's crisp and familiar details, Mrs. Radcliffe put the Miltonic and Burkean incomplete and sinister description, the face in the shadow, etc. Yet much more scenery was used. Unfamiliar and sensational settings and events were added. Contrasts of mood and contrasts or harmonies of scenery with mood were pointed out.

In general, Mrs. Radcliffe's novels aroused anxiety and curiosity by systematic developments of the passive, reacting protagonist, the static situation of danger, and the externally manipulated plot. The chief means of development was exaggeration of the number and nature of the stimuli. Almost every device she used played up a sensational, fear-creating contrast suggested by Burke (who had said that fear was the source of the sublime).[20]

I spoke earlier of Dickens's connection with the Gothic school, and it is obvious that there are Gothic elements even in his early novels, but it is important to note that *The Old Curiosity Shop,* Dickens's first novel done systematically in the Gothic manner, seems rather close to Mrs. Radcliffe's staple. *The Old Curiosity Shop* grew out of a plan for a short Gothic story. Dickens said "it [had been] always in my fancy to surround the lonely figure of the child with grotesque and wild, but not impossible companions, and to gather about her innocent face and pure intentions, associates as strange and uncongenial as the grim objects that are about her bed when her history is first foreshadowed."[21] A clearer statement of the intention to develop a sensational contrast could hardly be made. The statement is also a fairly complete description of the situation of the heroine in Mrs. Radcliffe's kind of Gothic novel (*Vathek, The Monk, Frankenstein, Melmoth the Wanderer* are different: they are male, Faustian, more seriously symbolic, and more supernatural). The heroine in danger, the announced and purposeful Gothic atmosphere, the announced and conscious concentration on romantic scenery as scenery are evidences of her influence. And there are larger numbers of sensational incidents in this and Dickens's later novels. Then, the rather Wordsworthian sentiments expressed in *The Old Curiosity Shop*[22] may actually be echoes of Mrs. Radcliffe, who expressed many of "Wordsworth's" ideas about nature before he did.[23]

From this time on, Dickens used techniques to arouse anxiety and curiosity systematically. The result was the creation of constant suspense, an odd fact, for Forster says that he found "suspense of any kind" "intolerable."[24] But then men often love and seek under one form what they hate in another. The serial has been famous ever since for suspense.

Devices producing anxiety are more fundamental than those producing curiosity, which is perhaps only a special kind of anxiety. Smollett in the preface to his semi-Gothic *Ferdinand, Count Fatham* had said that a hero was necessary to "unite the incidents [and], unwind the clue of the labyrinth."[25] Dickens eventually came to say in a letter to Collins that something bad could be shown the Victorian public only by picturing a girl victimized by it.[26] These remarks in a book by a novelist Dickens obviously imitated and in a letter probably indicate Dickens was conscious of the technique of arousing anxiety which he used.

In Dickens's use the passive protagonist[27] was trapped early in a novel in a large and rather static situation of danger and pain, usually quite cleverly worked out and quite believable. Then the protagonist was assaulted by incidents which momentarily embodied the danger and pain. The incidents were provided sometimes by hosts of minor villains or by personified aspects of some terrible contemporary social situation, and relief and perpetuation of the situation were provided by various kindly people who pitied the protagonist.

The most important part of this complex was the static situation of danger and pain. We can see its operation in *Dombey and Son*. At the start, Dickens tells of the birth of Dombey's son and then reveals the situation between Dombey and Florence. Dombey does not really appreciate her since she is a girl. Immediately we fear that Florence will be overshadowed by the boy. Then Dickens shows that Mrs. Dombey is failing. Our natural hope that Mrs. Dombey will get well is intensified by our anxiety that Florence will lead a very unhappy life if her mother dies. Mrs. Dombey dies. In the second chapter, Dickens concentrates on the provisions made for nursing the boy (Paul). This shift of his attention away from Florence becomes symbolic of what we fear others will do. In the third chapter of the book, Florence comes back to the house after an absence, and we are shown her grief at her mother's death and absence, which makes us more anxious about her happiness. Dombey is cold to her when she sees him for the first time after she gets back. Our anxiety mounts. Later we are shown that Dombey has become jealous of the affection Florence had got from her mother, and this, too, makes us anxious. In Chapter V, the next in which Florence appears, the unfeeling treatment of her by her father's sister and the sister's friend, Miss Tox, arouses more anxiety about Florence.

Our anxiety is raised again and again in succeeding incidents: in Chapter VI by Florence's capture by an old woman who steals her clothes; in Chapter VII by the revelation Miss Tox wants to be the second Mrs. Dombey; in Chapter VIII by the love which the weak but darling son shows Florence (which we know will do her no good); in Chapters VIII, IX, and X by the pushing of Florence into the background; in Chapter XI by Dombey's announcement to Mrs. Pipchin that he wishes to separate Paul from Florence; in the same chapter by the first step, Paul's going to school; in Chapter XIII by Dombey's ordering Walter Gay (Florence's friend) to the West Indies; in Chapter XVI by Paul's death, which we feel can do nothing but harm to Florence, though we are not sure how; and so on. Florence's situation is constantly changed on the surface, but basically is fixed: she yearns for her father's love while he withholds it and maltreats her. Every installment has elements which arouse anxiety and remind the reader about this basic situation. The clearest examples of this sort of organization are *Oliver Twist, Nicholas Nickleby* (in these the anxiety is not aroused constantly), *The Old Curiosity Shop, Martin Chuzzlewit, Dombey and Son, David Copperfield, Little Dorrit, Edwin Drood.*

Often there are in a novel several lesser, connecting static situations of danger about which we are reminded constantly by Dickens. For instance, in *Bleak House* we worry about Lady Dedlock's secret, about Richard's shiftlessness, about Esther's affection for Woodcourt, about George's debt, and several other things. Yet even when an incident does not fit into the basic situation, as when Florence is catured by the old woman who steals her clothes, that incident is connected with all others which have happened to the character for whom anxiety is aroused. It is connected by the anxiety and by the similarity of the incident, in effect, to others which are part of one of the static situations. Then, when a "bad" character acts in a way which does not at once seem connected with the basic situation, anxiety is also aroused in us, because we know what he has done in the past which has aroused our anxiety directly. Thus in *Dombey and Son* when

Carker begins to try to ensnare Edith, we become vaguely worried for Florence at once (as well as for other people less vaguely). We feel that this action bodes no good for Edith and Dombey or for their marriage and that in some way Carker is going to worm his way into the Dombey household and make Florence even more unhappy. Moreover, we feel this long before Carker has any success or the actual effect on Florence's life is revealed. Thus a whole novel can be organized around a static situation of pain and danger entrapping a passive protagonist.

Obviously many characters, and also places and events, become, in such an episodic plot, merely the stimuli for a protagonist. Yet since frequently the protagonist travels, as a kind of passive *pícaro,* the minor characters are often as fixed and static as the protagonist in his situation. Dickens, apparently because of his gradual revelation of different aspects of a character, was unaware of how true this was. He wrote Forster that it was odd that " 'Jeffrey should form his notion of Dombey and Miss Tox on three month's knowledge' " and that this tendency was a drawback of serial publication.[28]

The static situation of danger is set up by having people of different or clashing temperaments forced to live together, especially a passive sympathetic character and an active unsympathetic one, as in *Dombey and Son, David Copperfield, Hard Times, Little Dorrit,* and others. The more important part of this arrangement is the passive protagonist. Suffering children are fundamental to *Oliver Twist, The Old Curiosity Shop, Dombey and Son, David Copperfield,* and *Great Expectations* and suffering women to *Nicholas Nickleby, Barnaby Rudge, David Copperfield, Bleak House, Hard Times, Little Dorrit, A Tale of Two Cities, Our Mutual Friend,* and *Edwin Drood.* The male children and perhaps Florence (in *Dombey and Son*) and Lizzie (in *Our Mutual Friend*) are more interesting than most of Dickens's suffering females. The latter are often limp, little, cheerful, and saintly in ways repulsive to modern readers. The heroes are rather passive most of the time, too, but Dickens deepened his treatment of all his protagonists in time.

The second part of the static situation is the villain, but Dickens's antagonists are a variation from the Gothic novel in three ways. They often do only one or two things instead of a series. They often do nothing. They are often vague. Ralph Nickleby, Hugh, Pecksniff, Fagin, Carker, Mrs. Defarge, and Orlick are the closest to regular Gothic villains who will do anything evil. But instead of such extremists Dickens tends to use hosts of minor villains. The majority perform avaricious, malicious, fanatical, or simply female acts or combinations of those. They are brought onto the stage only now and then to move the plot forward. They are unpleasant enough when they are, but they are hardly organizing forces. Dorrit and Skimpole are examples. Many spend their time making villainous noises, but doing almost nothing. The most obvious example of this is Quilp. Many of Dickens's novels really have no villains, at least of the kind that kidnap ladies and boil people in oil. Most of his antagonistic characters are far more commonplace than those of some serial writers or than those of many Gothic novels.

In *Bleak House* and *Hard Times* the antagonists are larger than individuals; they are social forces or institutions with individuals employed as examples or tools. Hence Dickens is frequently vague about his villains. On the whole his novels seem the more realistic because of this vagueness. Nevertheless, in books so full of trouble and troublemakers (but intended to give

pleasure) superhuman, super-kind, reassuring characters or rescuers are very important. They serve as a
balance, and are providers of happy events (for relief)
and happy endings. Dickens uses many of them. Dickens gives people like Brownlow in *Oliver Twist* and
Jaggers in *Great Expectations* a sort of vague, limitless
(and apparently causeless) power of the kind with
which many an ignorant person invests a rich man or
a successful lawyer. Bucket, the detective in *Bleak
House*, has this power to an unusual degree. We can
see in him why Dickens's reassuring characters exude
power: they have experience and money and they act.
The effect is electric in books full of passive characters.
The reader in some cases has a tendency to identify
himself with the reassuring character more completely
than he does with the hero. It is no wonder that Bucket, the active detective who gradually solved a crime
and a second mystery, encouraged the pattern of the
modern detective-hero, and that Dickens's earlier
murder-mystery technique of merely letting the facts
be revealed gradually, as in *Barnaby Rudge,* has not
been imitated as much. These reassurers are also used
as supplementary connecting devices. Thus in *Bleak
House* Jarndyce's kindness to Esther, Woodcourt, Ada,
Richard, Charley, Skimpole, and others ties many of
the plot lines together.

c) *analyses of situations or events
from controlled points of view*

The Gothic anxiety helped Dickens combine his
careful arrangement of incident and his controlled
alternate advances of plots with realities of character
and social influence, but the novels still at times
seemed disconnected. Dickens had written two novels in which he introduced the Gothic techniques
for arousing curiosity and anxiety systematically,

The Old Curiosity Shop and *Barnaby Rudge*. After these, which had both appeared in a weekly periodical, he published a statement about the weekly serial. He explained that it was unfit as a method of publishing a novel (though he later returned to it), unfit because its interruptions made connections difficult. Of connections, he said: "Many passages in a tale of any length, depend materially for their interest on the intimate relation they bear to what has gone before, or to what is to follow."[29] So he understood the problem.

The second step in Dickens's increasing the role of the passive protagonist at first may not seem connected to protagonists at all: after the two rather Gothic novels mentioned above, Dickens's analyses of characters and subjects increased greatly in number and extent and in the amount of personal identification involved. Although the public never really appreciated the fact, Dickens's very next novel, *Martin Chuzzlewit*, devoted to the explorations of the various kinds of selfishness,[30] was a considerably more analytic book than any that had gone before.

In all of Dickens's novels there are hundreds of analyses of minor situations. Bumble's capitulation to his wife in *Oliver Twist*, for example, is analyzed; there are only one or two lines of direct explanation, and most of the situation is explained by carefully arranged actions. In the same novel the motivation of criminals is explored dramatically in the pictures of Fagin's gang. In his next novel, after briefer pictures of crime, Dickens sums up at least the youthful criminals' motivation by saying criminals have their own private worlds which they strive to please.[31] In the use of these short analyses Dickens is very clever. Consider the little picture of Jaggers's and Wemmick's embarrassment at Jaggers's revelation of his saving his maid's baby and at Pip's announcement that he has been to Wemmick's pleasant home. A few sentences of dialogue express the embarrassment. Dickens, through Pip, explains or analyzes it by saying that each felt he had been seen by the other in a nonprofessional light. Then in a short comic episode the feeling is removed by their reproving another man for unbusinesslike conduct. That is all there is. Yet we are shown a great deal about the relationship of Jaggers and Wemmick and a small part of the general problem of man and his relationship to money.[32] It is important to notice that these analyses are executed by Dickens's sympathetic identification with his characters, by his feeling what it is like to live their lives. These analyses are very brief and considerably more common in *Martin Chuzzlewit,* which had an analytic intention, and in later books than in the first novels.

A longer kind of analysis, that of a whole character, is rather rare in the books before *Martin Chuzzlewit,* except in *Oliver Twist,* which is obviously more earnest and reformist than the others. Virtually no major character analyses are in *Pickwick Papers* and *Nicholas Nickleby.* We can consider the treatments of Trent in *The Old Curiosity Shop* and of Chester and Gordon in *Barnaby Rudge* as attempts, but these are nothing like the extended studies of the boy criminals, of Sikes, and of Nancy in *Oliver Twist* until Pecksniff, Mercy, Tigg, Jonas, Mrs. Gamp and a host of others are exposed in their inmost workings in *Martin Chuzzlewit.* In almost all the novels thereafter, crowds of characters are so analyzed, especially in *Dombey and Son, David Copperfield, Hard Times, Little Dorrit, Great Expectations,* and *Our Mutual Friend* (in seven of the last ten novels, which include *Martin Chuzzlewit*). Furthermore, most of these analyses involve dramatic *incident,* though expository passages are often added. Yet a mere list of some of the most important will recall that these analyses are also dependent on Dickens's seeing himself in the characters' lives and that many of their most vivid moments occur as Dickens traces their thoughts and feelings. Certainly this method is apparent in the cases of Jonas, Dombey, Harthouse, Dorrit, and Headstone. Still others are captured for us because Dickens can imagine himself in close, passive association or family relationship, though not identification, with them, as in the cases of Tigg, Mrs. Gamp, Edith Dombey, Dora, Murdstone, Mrs. Clennam, Fanny Dorrit, Bella, Edwin Drood.

Analyses of subjects larger than one character, but usually associated with character, occur here and there in the early novels: the election at Eatanswill; the trial of Pickwick; the New Poor Law; the gang of boy criminals; Sikes's murder of Nancy, flight, and death; the Gordon Riots (though this last is often impersonal and is not altogether successful). Yet almost all of these are rather short—complete in one chapter or in a few chapters. Then, in *Martin Chuzzlewit*, we get a lengthy analysis of a crime. It is important that where a subject is analyzed in part of a novel, the part is developed, despite Dickens's love of variety, in such a way that the subject's analysis is at least not obscured. In *Martin Chuzzlewit* the murder is analyzed (dramatically) by the following development of the incident. In installment 11, Jonas is invited to join Tigg's phony company and is impressed by Tigg's display of wealth; also Tigg puts a detective on Jonas. In installment 14, Jonas, already in the company, is blackmailed into putting up more money and getting more victims, especially Pecksniff. In installment 15, Jonas's attempt to escape to the Continent is frustrated, and Jonas hears that Tigg is the only one who knows his secret (whatever it is). Also Jonas decides to kill Tigg when an accident gives him a chance to do it in a way which will appear accidental. Then Jonas leaves Tigg after persuading Pecksniff. In installment 17, Jonas misses his one chance of learning that he is watched (by the detective Nadgett), sets up an alibi, and commits the murder. Later installments show the law's closing in on Jonas. Other material occurs in these installments but that cannot obscure the fact that we have here a chain of causes and effects leading up to an important event and then tracing its consequences, including small but significant details and the means by which things are done—in short, a full analysis of a process. Again, this analysis depends upon an extended identification of Dickens and the reader with the chief character involved, Jonas Chuzzlewit. This identification is primarily caused by Dickens's looking at these incidents over Jonas's shoulder most of the time.

Most of the later novels are devoted as totals to the analyses of, as well as allegories upon, large subjects. In *Dombey and Son,* we see pride as a poison destroying marital and filial relationships. In *David Copperfield,* we learn about the value of the heart, the weakness in family and business of those with undisciplined hearts (David's mother, David, Dora, Micawber, Em'ly, and others), and the destructiveness of the heartless (Murdstone, Creakle, the Steerforths, Heep, etc.). In *Bleak House,* we see the dead hand of the law, and in *Hard Times,* we see the results of thorough application of classical economics. And so on. The reader may find the analysis and demonstration lagging behind the allegory and symbolic assertion in *Hard Times* and one or two others, but both are there. Moreover, as before, these are personal analyses conducted not like the impersonal studies of an academician but from the points of view of various individuals involved with these huge subjects and conducted by means of tracing their reactions to the subjects. This increased interest in analysis from the point of view of usually passive persons involved made a contribution, then, to Dickens's increasing of the role of the passive protagonist in ways that should be clear enough. The actual connection is made in the next step.

d) *the fully biographical approach*

The third step in Dickens's increasing of the role of the passive protagonist was his increasing use of the fully biographical approach and the narrowing in point of view which accompanied this. Dickens's early novels were biographical in a sense. *Nicholas Nickleby* is in its very name reminiscent of Smollett and the long, eighteenth-century tradition of loose, varied, semi-biographical novels. This kind of story Dickens kept up for quite a while. Such story is not mature plotting and it is not really biography. A few months of Pickwick's adult life are given; the same is true of Nicholas Nickleby, Barnaby Rudge (though an interval of five years is skipped), and Martin Chuzzlewit. And in *The Old Curiosity Shop* a few weeks in the life of a child are shown. *Oliver Twist* does begin with the birth of its protagonist, but the time span of most of the story is only a few months and he has not ceased to be a child at the end of the story.

Dombey and Son and later novels follow a clearer biographical pattern. Florence Dombey grows from a child to an adult. David Copperfield, Esther Summerson, Louisa Gradgrind, Little Dorrit, and Pip all do the same. The advantage of this pattern is, that since the growing person in these truly biographical novels is usually the protagonist in some sense, the protagonist is involved directly or indirectly in most of the events and the novel consists of the experiences of the protagonist.

Now it happens that Forster's remarks about *David Copperfield* show that Dickens thought of experiences as stimuli assaulting a passive being. Forster discusses Dickens's intentions in regard to *David Copperfield* and remarks on unautobiographical portions of the novel. He says (and, as so often, appears to be echoing Dickens or quoting him indirectly): "Take autobiography as a design to show that any man's life may be as a mirror of existence to all men, and the individual career becomes altogether secondary to the variety of experiences *received* and rendered back in it [my italics]."[33] The biographical approach then involved an extension of the passive protagonist. Faced by the adventures of earlier passive protagonists like Nell and Martin Chuzzlewit, the reader could complain with some justice that Dickens did finger exercises with variations of the static situation of pain and danger entrapping the protagonist. The reader could charge that Dickens maneuvered events and stimuli unnaturally from outside. For protagonists who were shown growing up in relation to a static situation of pain and danger, however, the procession of stimuli, even if fairly disparate, seemed the realistic and organic accumulation of experience by a passive receiver.

The biographical approach also led to a restriction of point of view in a technical sense. In the biographical novels Dickens employs his usual technique of looking over the shoulder of the most important character in the individual chapter. Moreover, in these books that is often the hero. So he attains something like a restricted third-person point of view. It is not really that, however, because he judges actions, analyzes characters, and predicts events—occasionally. This point of view also contributes to the sense of unity gained from the hero's participation in most of the events. The effect is intensified in those books told in the first person, *David Copperfield, Bleak House* (or a large part of it), and *Great Expectations.*

When Dickens combines a story about a passive protagonist's whole life and a static situation and a single point of view or when he combines just two of these, the unity he attains is something much more profound than the mere dragging of the reader from installment to installment by means of anxiety. Dickens told Forster in regard to *A Tale of Two Cities*, " 'I set myself the little task of making *a picturesque story* . . . with characters . . . whom the story should express more than they should express themselves by dialogue. . . . I fancied a story of incident might be written . . . pounding the characters in its own mortar, and beating their interest out of them.' "[34] Forster said of the book that he knew of no novel "in which the domestic life of a few simple, private people is in such a manner knitted and interwoven with the outbreak of a terrible public event, that the one seems but a part of the other."[35] Perhaps Forster was unfamiliar with the great war novels of his century, some of which were written by this time. It is characteristic of Dickens to think of the sympathetic individuals as passive no matter what changes he made in his method. His anticipation of the naturalistic war or poverty novels of the twentieth century has not always been noticed, however. In *A Tale of Two Cities,* the French Revolution is pictured so vividly and convincingly as an enormous force that the passive characters and the coincidences and the tyings together of apparently unrelated events seem real. Dickens's ideas that man was passive and the world hostile and aggressive particularly fitted the French Revolution. So did his frequent use of offstage action. Jackson says "the main action emerges as something over and beyond all the subsidiary actions, as the positive outcome of their *interaction*."[36]

The same sort of effect may have been sought in *Barnaby Rudge*. The first half is a story about individuals. In the second half they are shown involved in a social upheaval, the Gordon Riots.[37] I feel the domestic first half is insufficiently connected to the account of the riots and that the deeds of violence seem much the same (as they were in fact). Still, even if imperfectly, the book achieves the unity of mood which a huge and overpowering basic situation can give. But it is worth noting that the situation when so huge is shown to be slowly changing and to cause changes in the characters to some extent.

The first-person point of view adds another unifying factor. Miss Needham emphasizes the importance of retrospect in *David Copperfield*.[38] Retrospect is really an extremely narrowed point of view. Even an autobiography *can* be told as if each new chapter were happening right now. Moreover, the presentation of first one aspect of a character and then another for artful impressionistic effect also occurs in *David Copperfield*. It is retrospect which combines the variety and the unity.

The results are amazing, for in this book the intense focus on one small area after another seems more natural. This is what retrospect is like for many: spots of emotionally charged material. And childhood is an impressionistic piecing together of bits of a pattern, later clearer. The emotional load of Dickens's material, the personal view of the world as hell and man as a passive victim of it, seems more natural. Memories are often overdramatic and exaggerated. Often children seem or feel passive and seem or feel or are subjected to hell. Even the rogue-story element seems

natural in a child, for allegiances may b(
fairly late. So the child-hero and the chil(
this novel, as in *Great Expectations* and M(
Huckleberry Finn,[39] make an hysterical, th(
and idealistic, view of the world seem accep(......
emotional and philosophic postures of the author have
been in a precise and constant relationship (and near-
identity) with those of the hero. Dickens achieves this
again in *Great Expectations*, where he also causes the
reader for a time to accept his total view of the world.

e) the focus upon psychological reform

The fourth and final step in Dickens's increasing
of the role of the passive protagonist was his extension
of the passive protagonist's growing up in the neighbor-
hood of a static situation of pain and danger. He expanded this growing up in order to include the protagonist's being pushed by experience into an emotional reform. The history of his adoption of this device was
full of contradictory movement because the picture
ultimately desired was of a human being in profound
conflict. In *Oliver Twist* and the novels just following
it, the characters of whom Dickens painted powerful
and sympathetic portraits tended to be villains while
his general sympathy came more and more to be extended to a passive protagonist victim. Then in *Martin
Chuzzlewit* Dickens began to fuse on a thematic level
his sympathies for villains and victims. The brilliant
picture of Jonas from one point of view and the critical
but unconvincing picture of the originally selfish Martin were the result.

The plan of the next novel carried the process
further. An emotional change was to occur in Dombey's domestic relationships after a series of events
caused a catastrophe.[40] The moral criticism of individual conduct noted in the Christmas Books and visible

in the plot of *Martin Chuzzlewit* is pronounced in this *plan*. And from Florence's point of view Dombey is a villain of a kind. The original covers for *Dombey and Son* seem, however, to emphasize the downfall of Dombey's firm.[41] So the book started with two somewhat divergent plans, as it were. The book lives up to neither very well. Dombey's character causes certain actions which produce certain events which cause his downfall and eventual change of heart. This part of the plot is good, but the study of his changing heart which is virtually promised by the general plan and the decided business slant promised by the covers are never really delivered. The changes in Dombey occur largely in a few brief passages of direct exposition and at the very end of the book, for Dombey, unlike many earlier hard-hearted characters is rather static. Also much of the interest is switched to Florence, whose mind is not explored. The main plan, which involves an analysis of Dombey, is not used and does not govern the technical treatment of the story except in a very few places. The letter to Forster had outlined a vague, general domestic emotional process, happening to Dombey. It was rather somber, but warmer and more concrete than that reform in part of *Martin Chuzzlewit* and was like nothing so much as the changes in Scrooge and in Pip in *Great Expectations*. It was unlike *Great Expectations*, however, in that the plan here is more convincing and powerful than its working out.

David Copperfield moved in the opposite direction. It is about the education and disciplining of a soft heart (David's).[42] Every feeling of the protagonist is still followed with great sympathy, but David is often laughed at, and many of his feelings prove to be the causes of calamities. This book is an important development, for it involves effective criticism of the passive victim, whereas the previous novel had involved the first fairly extended softening of a rather static villain.

In *Hard Times* these two aspects are merged in the cool treatment of Louisa, who wakes up to reality, and in the picture of her father and his associates. Yet only part of the domestic portion of *Hard Times* is devoted to the effects of Gradgrind's teachings. Moreover, Dickens merely suggests what the effects are and avoids showing how they came about as a result of the teachings. Stephen's story, Bounderby, and Mrs. Sparsit get too much space for the book to be effectively organized around the results of Gradgrind's teaching, though there is some tendency that way. Dickens intended Bounderby's and Gradgrind's actions and philosophies to be related, but did not suceed in making them wholly so.[43]

It is true that the economic creation of the hard Louisa is not very convincing. But this flaw should not blind us to the fact that such steps in the important process of reform as the attraction of rebellion (in the form of Harthouse) are made in dramatically powerful and psychologically convincing ways. By way of *David Copperfield* Dickens had come a step beyond the explained reforms of Dombey and *Dombey and Son's* outlined chain of events which sweep along only when other parts of the book are dropped from the mind.

Finally, in *Great Expectations*, all the aspects of reform and all the four methods of exploring a passive protagonist are combined in the history of a single character. The result is a novel which in many ways is the peak of Dickens's achievement. The situation of danger and the biography are fused, for the huge, almost static situation becomes that stage of growing up in which one is slowly swept from the undesirable cramping of childhood to the subtler pressures of adult temptation. This is really a final fusion of the device of the static situation with the picaresque story. Dickens's stories of traveling youngsters had been transformed so that in the later novels the physical area covered was often much smaller and the kind of travel was often more abstract, closer to mental change, as in *Dombey and Son, David Copperfield, Little Dorrit, Our Mutual Friend.* The passive reacting hero is moved slowly over a big or little canvas, but the view is always of things outside the hero which stimulate or pressure him. In *Great Expectations* the idea of enormous change and mental travel or reform makes sense as the experience of an adolescent. The journey has been analyzed and arranged until it has become the journey of life; the contrasts, shocks, ironies, hopes, jokes, sights, people being those of life and one's family and one's striving.

All of this has been merged with a convincing reform plot, because the protagonist fuses the best of Dickens's sympathetic villains and satirized heroes. The sensibility novels, from 1740 to 1840 or later, had been written and read in the humble faith that learning to react vigorously and unrestrainedly to events and people and things was a way of developing Christian love and virtue, a way of becoming refined and aristocratic, even at times a way of reaching God and the truth by the development of a natural and moral part of the personality. These novels, as well as plays and poems (like *The Rime of the Ancient Mariner*) of a similar kind, often show a hard, unreacting and hence evil man, being softened by misfortune and hence made good (the metaphor is in the *Psalms* and many other places). At their worst these novels suggest the advantages of a sensibility so extreme as to be idiotic. Dickens had shared the faith in sensibility and had used the motif over and over again, though with increasing modification and depth. Yet, like Smollett in *Humphry Clinker,* he was able finally in *Great Ex-*

pectations to suggest the place of sensibility in the life of all men in all ages. He limited the power, point, and display of sensibility by drawing a man whose sensibility was not just an enormous sensational and sentimental contrast to that of all men around him, but a mere part of his character and a close parallel to the amount and kind of sensibility in the life of an actual man, with a good bit of selfishness to balance it.

The hero is still fairly passive on the surface, though he is aggressive emotionally in his ambition. Dickens's technique is refined here, but still is really the procession of stimuli. The first-person narrative and very careful selection make them seem likely to cause changes of the kind gradually indicated by very slight changes in Pip's behavior. The variety and alternation of incident become here the variety and contradiction of experience occurring to a complex protagonist who is at first a compound of love and pride, of sensitivity and hardness. The contradictory experience causes pain but gradually knocks away the pride and makes possible an adult acceptance of and union with the world, thus leading ultimately to joy.

Lastly, the fictional analysis of these matters is central, and all extraneous material is cut away. Pip's kindness to a criminal and his humble background are shown right away. Next we are told of his introduction to Estella, his sensitivity about his low station, and his half-successful efforts to better himself. Pip's mind has been shown developing to the point where it will be most receptive to wealth, or rather stimuli which would reasonably develop it to that point have been shown (his mind is not really shown much). Then he is told his great expectations. He becomes proud and expects Estella's hand. He gads about London. Then Magwitch comes home, and all Pip's castles fall. He decides not to touch Magwitch's money (or petition for it after it is forfeited) and eventually meets Estella again (now also humbled). The development is fairly steady; one event is based on another, and all are based on character. The order, the rate, and the rhythm of the story are parallel to what we find in life when we get our hopes up unreasonably and parallel to adolescence in general. The result is a profound, though perhaps quiet, emotional response to the story.

It is a unified, carefully shaped novel on the dangers of having fairy godmothers (who are considered good in Dickens's other novels). The inclusion of the reform motif tempers the pessimism of the casting away of rescue (which also involves a passive sympathetic character).

All four devices for exploring the passive protagonist help produce our response. We fear for Pip, as criminals, relatives, social aggressors and pressures enter his life, and as he makes some missteps in response. The distinct parts of his psychological history are kept before our eyes as are their relations to his life as a whole. A wealth of detail is presented and convincing, emotionally colored lights are cast upon it by the retrospective telling, so that we can well accept the story as the biography of a real person. The psychological reform takes place so gradually and from such a believable beginning to such a believable end and with such lifelike modifications that it seems something we ourselves have been through.

When we reflect that *Great Expectations* preserves all the humor and high adventure of *Pickwick Papers*, while having achieved at least these four new values, we may be glad that Dickens decided to explore the passive protagonist, for his decision led on to a series of novels with new greatness, and to the gradual development of an art with more intimacy and more passion.

Great Expectations succeeds in merging the symbolic world of Dickens's vision, the alternating plot, the imitation of a process, and all the complex techniques involved in these. We may say, then, that Dickens had the great structural challenge of serial plotting solved by the time of the general plan for *Dombey and Son,* but that he continued to improve his solution until *Great Expectations.*

Literary critics have been accustomed to treat the serial with scorn, but we have seen that Dickens associated it with his success. The association was not merely a sentimental clinging to the method of *Pickwick* (Dickens came to think less of that novel). Nor was it merely the semi-dramatic interaction with his audience which made the association pleasant and important. No. The serial with its monumental problems challenged a man of strong feeling, clear vision, immense imagination, and boundless energy. However much some may disagree with his feelings and vision, none can deny that he wrote and wrote and wrote, confronting the serial again and again. He saw its problems and mentioned them to others—only on minor points ever suggesting those problems were different from the problems of the novel in general. He worked and worked to solve each of them, and, as excited letters about *Dombey and Son, Great Expectations,* and other novels show, he saw that he overcame them. Challenged by the vastness and immediacy of serial writing, his imaginative vision lifted him over all obstacles and swept him to brilliant achievements. Jonas Chuzzlewit's murder and attempted escape; the marriage between those two proud, wounded spirits, Dombey and Edith; the rapprochement between Pip and Magwitch, tender, but never sentimental; these and many events in the novels sweep through many installments. Dickens's treatment with its symbolic suggestiveness, its profound conflict, and psychological process compels us to accept them as unified visions, as we do the novels themselves. But these pictures are better and fuller than they would have been without serialization. The symbolism is more extensive, the suspense is more constant, the psychology is tighter than any of these would ever have been in an ordinary novel. For these and other triumphs, hundreds of writers have studied his work. Yet there is something they, avoiding serials, can never hope to recapture. By means of complex mechanical devices, Dickens was able to harness the size and rapid change and variety of the serial itself and use it to express in organic unity his own extraordinary and colorful view of life. And so the serial became part of that tender, cheap, subtle, explosive mystery that was Dickens.

NOTES TO TEXT

Chapter 1

THE ARTISTIC SIGNIFICANCE
OF SERIAL DISTORTION

1. A detailed account of Dickens's impact on other writers and upon the public is to be found in G. Ford, *Dickens and His Readers: Aspects of Novel-Criticism Since 1836* (Princeton, 1955).

2. A brief discussion of this attitude and the related critical debate, as well as a beginning bibliography of the subject by Inglis Bell, are in the "Introduction" to Inglis F. Bell and Donald Baird, *The English Novel: A Checklist of Twentieth-Century Criticism* (Denver, 1958), pp. ix, x, xii.

3. John Forster, *The Life of Charles Dickens*, ed. J. W. T. Ley (New York, 1927), p. 720.

4. Forster, p. 111.

5. Letter to Collins written by Dickens in 1866 which is quoted in Jack Lindsay, *Charles Dickens: A Biographical and Critical Study* (New York, 1950), pp. 357–58.

6. Forster, pp. 472–73.

7. Many such letters are quoted by W. C. Phillips, *Dickens, Reade, and Collins, Sensation Novelists* (New York, 1919) and Monroe Engel, *The Maturity of Dickens* (Cambridge, Mass., 1959).

8. Edmund Wilson's long and penetrating essay "Dickens: The Two Scrooges," *The Wound and the Bow* (New York, 1941) employs something like this method, combining it with

biographical materials. Of the books that employ it, alone or with other matter and other methods, the following are among the most important: T. A. Jackson, *Charles Dickens: The Progress of a Radical* (London, 1937); the individual works by Forster, Engel, and Lindsay mentioned above; Edgar Johnson, *Charles Dickens: His Tragedy and Triumph* (New York, 1952); J. Hillis Miller, *Charles Dickens: The World of His Novels* (Cambridge, Mass., 1958).

   9. I have attempted to show that Dickens's vision had an overall philosophic (Transcendental) organization. See "Dickens and the Philosophic Basis of Melodrama" and "Dickens and the Heart as the Hope for Heaven: A study of the philosophic basis of sensational literary technique," *Victorian Newsletter,* No. 20 (Fall, 1961), pp. 1–6 and 6–13. The reader will also find, in Chapter 5 and Appendix 2, discussion of Dickens's symbolic patterns, especially their repeated elements. Other discussions are to be found in the works by Wilson, Lindsay, and Miller mentioned above.

Chapter 4

SOME TEMPTATIONS
OF SERIAL COMPOSITION

   1. This Preface is quoted in John Butt and Kathleen Tillotson, *Dickens at Work* (Flair Lawn, New Jersey, 1958), pp. 62–64.
   2. G. Grubb, "Dickens' Pattern of Weekly Serialization," *ELH,* IX (1942), 141–56.
   3. John Butt, "David Copperfield: From Manuscript to Print," *The Review of English Studies,* New Series, I, No. 3 (July, 1950), 247–51; Grubb, 141–56; John Forster, *The Life of Charles Dickens,* ed. J. W. T. Ley (New York, 1927), p. 730; Edgar Johnson, *Charles Dickens: His Tragedy and Triumph* (New York, 1952), II, 950.
   4. K. J. Fielding, "Charles Dickens and the Department of Practical Art," *The Modern Language Review,* XLVIII, No. 3 (July, 1953), 275.
   5. Quoted in Forster, p. 437.
   6. Forster, p. 810.
   7. *Dickens at Work,* especially Chapters I, V, VI, and VIII.
   8. Fielding, p. 273.
   9. Forster, pp. 425–31, 443, 471–85.
   10. Quoted in Forster, p. 165.
   11. Forster, pp. 472–73.
   12. Forster, p. 808.
   13. *Dickens at Work,* p. 15.
   14. M. Joseph and M. Cumberland, *How to Write Serial Fiction* (New York, 1928), p. 22.
   15. See Note 2, Appendix 3, on divisions. For a case study of the relations of one writer to Dickens as an editor of a

magazine which published serials, see A. B. Hopkins, *Elizabeth Gaskell* (London, 1952), pp. 139–55.

16. Grubb, p. 153.

Chapter 5

A WORLD IN A BOOK

1. This chapter had been completed, and a manuscript of which it was a part had been submitted to a publisher when there appeared in the September, 1963, issue of *PMLA* William Axton's brilliant article "Tonal Unity in *Dombey and Son*" which applies this principle of the overlapping and unifying symbol to that novel in great and convincing detail.

2. Charles Dickens, *Oliver Twist, The Works of Charles Dickens,* "Collier's Unabridged Edition," P. F. Collier (New York [no date]), Preface, p. 1. The statement is not in the Gadshill edition.

The Preface to *Barnaby Rudge,* 1841, quoted in John Butt and Kathleen Tillotson, *Dickens at Work* (Fair Lawn, New Jersey, 1958), p. 82.

On *Martin Chuzzlewit,* see John Forster, *The Life of Charles Dickens,* ed. J. W. T. Ley (New York, 1927), p. 291. Here Forster is presumably quoting Dickens indirectly.

On *Dombey and Son,* see Forster, 471–73.

On *Hard Times,* see Humphry House, *The Dickens World* (Oxford, 1941), pp. 204, 205.

On *Little Dorrit,* see Forster, p. 625.

Charles Dickens, *A Tale of Two Cities,* p. xiii (Gadshill edition).

On *Great Expectations,* see Forster, pp. 733–34.

On *Edwin Drood,* see Forster, p. 808.

3. A similar kind of spatial pattern in more recent literature is discussed in Joseph Frank, "Spatial Form in Modern Literature," *Criticism, the Foundations of Modern Literary Judgment,* ed. Mark Schorer and others (New York, 1948), pp. 379–91.

4. Forster, p. 291.

5. See Forster, p. 627, and Lionel Trilling "Little Dorrit," *The Kenyon Review* (Gambier, Ohio) XV, No. 4 (Autumn, 1953), 577–90. See also Clennam's hint, *Little Dorrit,* I, 108. All references in my book to Dickens's novels, unless otherwise stated are to the Gadshill edition, ed. A. Lang, London, 1897–1908, 1911.

6. Forster mentions a hatred of religious forms—see Forster, pp. 173, 820. Dickens's agreement with Thomas Arnold on religious matters (see Forster, p. 350) is further evidence of a hatred of religious forms, for Arnold hated them, too (*Library of Universal Knowledge* [a reprint of the 1880 edition of Chamber's *Encyclopedia*], New York, 1880, I, 713–14, article on Arnold).

7. Forster, p. 347.

8. For her detailed discussion, see Kathleen Tillotson, *Novels of the Eighteen-Forties* (Oxford, 1956), pp. 150–56.

9. See Forster, p. 353. See James Morier, *The Adventures of Hajji Baba of Ispahan* (London, 1949), pp. 2, 3, 71, 283, 318.

10. This chapter had been completed, and a manuscript of which it was a part had been submitted to a publisher when Earle Davis's book *The Flint and the Flame* (Columbia, Missouri, 1963) appeared. In his book (pp. 148–49) Davis sees the Christmas Books as an influence pressing Dickens toward unity of structure, and demonstrates that their childish, moralistic, fairy tale aspects derive from the chapbooks. Dibelius had mentioned this derivation. On the designing of the Christmas Books for one reading, see Forster, pp. 353 and 438–39.

11. Forster, p. 290.

12. Jack Lindsay, *Charles Dickens: A Biographical and Critical Study* (New York, 1950), p. 241. In fact Lindsay makes the remark in a section which treats the Christmas Books, not the short stories.

13. Lindsay, p. 244.

14. Forster, p. 317.

15. Forster, pp. 317, 318.

16. T. A. Jackson, *Charles Dickens: The Progress of a Radical* (London, 1937), p. 287.

17. Charles Dickens, "Frauds on the Fairies," *The Works of Charles Dickens*, National Library Edition (New York [undated]),XVIII, I, 393. This edition is hereafter referred to as NLE.

18. NLE, XVIII, I, 393.

19. Forster, p. 515.

20. Dickens, "The Amusements of the People: I," NLE, XVIII, I, 118–24.

21. Dickens, "The Amusements of the People: II," NLE, XVIII, I, 126–32.

22. Forster, p. 622.

23. Lindsay, p. 325. For detailed discussion of the play, see Lindsay, pp. 323–25.

24. G. R. Stange, "Expectations Well Lost, Dickens' Fable for His Time," *College English*, ed. W. W. Hatfield (Champaign, Ill.) XVI, No. 1 (October, 1954), 9–17.

25. *Novels of the Eighteen-Forties*, p. 200. For her full discussion, see pp. 196–200.

26. Forster, p. 560.

Chapter 7

THE SERIAL'S DEMAND FOR ADVANCE

1. Quoted in John Butt and Kathleen Tillotson, *Dickens at Work* (Fair Lawn, New Jersey, 1958), p. 65.

2. *Pickwick Papers*, I, xiii.

3. Quoted in *Dickens at Work*, p. 124.

4. John Forster, *The Life of Charles Dickens*, ed. J. W. T. Ley (New York, 1927), p. 152; see also pp. 145–51.

5. Forster, p. 24.
6. Forster, pp. 733–34.
7. *Pickwick Papers*, I, xvi-xvii.
8. Forster, p. 152.
9. Forster, pp. 290–91.
10. Forster, p. 290; and Dickens's Preface quoted in Kathleen Tillotson, *Novels of the Eighteen-Forties* (Oxford, 1956), p. 42.
11. Forster, p. 302.
12. Forster, p. 294.
13. The developed structural contrasts are described at length in *Dickens at Work*, pp. 114–76. Dickens's hesitation is described by Forster, p. 536.
14. *Dickens at Work*, p. 214.
15. Forster, p. 625.
16. Forster, p. 625.
17. Forster, pp. 625–26.
18. As in *Little Dorrit*, I, 281 and II, 275.
19. *Little Dorrit*, Book I, Chapters 6, 8, 19, 31, 35, 36.

Chapter 8
SYMBOLIC ALTERNATION

1. Dickens, "The Amusements of the People: I and II," National Library Edition of Dickens's Works, XVIII, I, 118–24, 126–32, esp. 126–32.
2. *Oliver Twist*, Gadshill edition, ed. A. Lang, London, 1897–1908, 1911, pp. 146–47. Unless otherwise stated, later references to Dickens's novels are to this edition.
3. *Nicholas Nickleby*, I, 367.
4. John Forster, *The Life of Charles Dickens*, ed. J. W. T. Ley (New York, 1927), p. 45.
5. Forster, pp. 108–9.
6. Forster, p. 76.
7. Fred W. Boege, "Point of View in Dickens," *PMLA*, LXVI, No. 2 (March, 1950), 103.
8. See Ford Madox Ford's definition and discussion of impressionism in his *Joseph Conrad: A Personal Remembrance* (London, 1924), pp. 180–93, 207–10. Ford compares serial technique and impressionism on p. 207.
9. Sir Walter Scott, "Mrs. Ann Radcliffe," *The Lives of the Novelists*, Everyman's Library, ed. Ernest Rhys (New York [no date]), pp. 224, 227–29, 244.
10. Scott, p. 215.
11. Scott, p. 226, Note 1, and p. 231.
12. Samuel C. Chew, "The Nineteenth Century and After," *A Literary History of England*, ed. A. C. Baugh (New York, 1948), pp. 1266 (and Note 5 there), 1267.
13. R. D. Mayo, "Gothic Romances in the Magazines," *PMLA*, LXV, No. 5 (Sept., 1950), 762–89.
14. Ann Radcliffe, *The Italian* (1797), Ch. 15.
15. *The Italian*, Ch. 17.

16. John Butt and Kathleen Tillotson, *Dickens at Work* (Fair Lawn, New Jersey, 1958), p. 82.

17. *Dickens at Work*, p. 80.

18. *Barnaby Rudge*, I, 367.

19. *Barnaby Rudge*, II, 116.

20. On truth as stranger than fiction, see Forster, p. 135. On all men as secrets, see *Martin Chuzzlewit*, II, 37; *Hard Times*, p. 77; *A Tale of Two Cities*, pp. 12–13.

21. William Hazlitt, "On Imitation," available in W. J. Bate's anthology *Criticism: The Major Texts* (New York, 1952), p. 298.

22. See the letter called "The First Detective" by Joan Bryant in *TLS*, May 1, 1948.

23. The best discussion of the Dickens-Collins relationship is Chapter X of Earle Davis's *The Flint and the Flame* (Columbia, Missouri, 1963).

24. For other examples, see *Martin Chuzzlewit*, II, 323–24 and *Great Expectations*, p. 130.

25. *Dombey and Son*, II, 73.

26. J. H. Hagan describes a pattern something like this in *Great Expectations*. See his article, "Structural Patterns in Dickens's *Great Expectations*," *ELH*, ed. E. T. Norris (Baltimore) XXI (1954), 54–66.

27. Forster, p. 405.

28. Forster, pp. 472–73.

29. There is a full discussion of this incident in G. Grubb, "Dickens' Pattern of Weekly Serialization," *ELH*, IX (1942), 147–48, 151.

30. The introduction of Tartar, with whom Rosa is enthusiastically associated, has little to do with the mystery or its cause in the love triangle, for Tartar is a new character.

31. Forster describes the manuscript:

". . . a scene in which Sapsea the auctioneer is introduced as the principal figure, among a group of characters new to the story . . . perhaps . . . having become a little nervous about the course of the tale, from a fear that he might have plunged too soon into the incidents leading on to the catastrophe, such as the Datchery assumption in the fifth number (a misgiving he certainly expressed to his sister-in-law), it had occurred to him to open some fresh veins of character incidental to the interest, though not directly part of it, and so to handle them in connection with Sapsea as a little to suspend the final development even while assisting to strengthen it."

Forster quotes part of the notes to the first number of *Edwin Drood*: " 'Mr. Sapsea. Old Tory jackass. Connect Jasper with him. (he will want a solemn donkey by and by) [*sic*]' " See Forster, pp. 810 and 811–15 (which quote the additional passage entire).

32. *Our Mutual Friend*, II, 501–2.

Chapter 10
SERIAL INTERRUPTION OF PROCESS

1. For detailed discussion of these matters, see Kathleen Tillotson, *Novels of the Eighteen-Forties* (Oxford, 1956), pp. 39–41; Ellis N. Gummer, *Dickens' Works in Germany, 1837–1937* (Oxford, 1940), pp. 29–32; G. H. Ford, *Dickens and His Readers: Aspects of Novel-Criticism Since 1836* (Princeton, 1955), pp. 36, 123, 127, 128; A. B. Hopkins, *Elizabeth Gaskell: Her Life and Works* (London, 1952), pp. 137–55.
2. Ford, pp. 36, 123.
3. *Oliver Twist,* Gadshill edition, ed. A. Lang, London, 1897–1908, 1911, p. 124. Later references to Dickens's novels are to this edition unless otherwise noted.
4. On businessmen as schemers, see *Nicholas Nickleby,* I, 147, 154, for instance.
5. *Oliver Twist,* p. 236.
6. In *Pickwick Papers, Barnaby Rudge, David Copperfield, Little Dorrit,* and *A Tale of Two Cities,* for instance.
7. John Butt and Kathleen Tillotson, *Dickens at Work* (Fair Lawn, New Jersey, 1958), pp. 178–99.
8. *Dickens at Work,* pp. 210, 212.

Chapter 11
IDENTIFICATION WITH A
MATURING PASSIVE PROTAGONIST

1. See John Forster, *The Life of Charles Dickens,* ed. J. W. T. Ley (New York, 1927), pp. 88–89, 111, 120–21, 127, 149, 151, 348, 356, 420, 423, 424, 636, 762, 829.
2. See G. M. Kahrl, *Tobias Smollett, Traveller-Novelist* (Chicago, 1945).
3. See Forster, pp. 523–24.
4. Forster, p. 165.
5. Forster, p. 291.
6. Forster, p. 471.
7. Forster, pp. 472–73.
8. Forster, p. 405.
9. Forster, p. 810; pp. 810–14 describe and quote this extra scene to *Edwin Drood.*
10. Quoted in John Butt and Kathleen Tillotson, *Dickens at Work* (Fair Lawn, New Jersey, 1958), p. 88.
11. Forster, p. 311.
12. Forster, p. 111.
13. Forster, p. 350.
14. Forster, p. 353.
15. Forster, p. 721.
16. See *Dickens at Work,* pp. 114–76, esp. 143, 157, 161, 168, 169.

17. Sir Walter Scott, "Mrs. Ann Radcliffe," *The Lives of the Novelists,* Everyman's Library, ed. Ernest Rhys (New York [no date]), p. 225.

18. Scott, p. 215.

19. Scott, p. 226, Note 1, and p. 231.

20. See the discussion of Burke by George Wiley Sherburn, "The Restoration and the Eighteenth Century (1660–1789)," *A Literary History of England,* ed. A. C. Baugh (New York, 1948), p. 986.

21. Charles Dickens, Preface to *The Old Curiosity Shop* in the "First Cheap Edition," *The Works of Charles Dickens,* National Library Edition (New York [no date]), V, xi-xii.

22. As in *The Old Curiosity Shop,* Gadshill edition, ed. A. Lang, London, 1897–1908, 1911, I, 238–39 (compare *Oliver Twist,* Ch. XXXII). Later references to Dickens's novels are to this edition unless otherwise noted.

23. In Ann Radcliffe, *The Italian* (1797) the heroine is revived by nature in Ch. 6. In Ch. 8 her soul is strengthened and refreshed by landscape, and she sees God behind the landscape which he made and which is a "veil" or his "imagery"; she dwells "as with a present GOD," and man shrinks before nature.

24. Forster, p. 87.

25. Quoted by Sherburn, *A Literary History of England,* p. 961.

26. Quoted in Jack Lindsay, *Charles Dickens: A Biographical and Critical Study* (New York, 1950), pp. 357–58.

27. The general idea of the passive protagonist and the static situation of persecution as the basis of much serial plotting came to my attention through the section on radio serials by Mona Kent, in *Radio and Television Writing,* ed. M. Wylie (New York, 1950).

28. Forster, p. 480.

29. Quoted in *Dickens at Work,* pp. 88–89.

30. Forster, p. 291.

31. *Nicholas Nickleby,* I, 431–32.

32. *Great Expectations,* pp. 480–84. For other little analyses, see *The Old Curiosity Shop,* I, 355–56; *David Copperfield,* II, 55, 58, 59, 64; *Little Dorrit,* II, 164–66, 174; *Great Expectations,* pp. 15, 70–71, 74, 292.

33. Forster, p. 554.

34. Forster, p. 730.

35. Forster, pp. 731–32.

36. T. A. Jackson, *Charles Dickens: The Progress of a Radical* (London, 1937), p. 202.

37. *Dickens at Work,* p. 87.

38. See Gwendolyn B. Needham, "The Undisciplined Heart of David Copperfield," *NCF,* ed. B. A. Booth (Berkeley, Calif.) IX, No. 2 (Sept., 1954), 83–85.

39. There are extensive parallels between Twain's biography and philosophy and literary sources and methods and Dickens's, it seems to me. And the American scenes of *Martin Chuzzlewit* are rather like scenes in *Huckleberry Finn.*

40. Forster, pp. 472–73.

41. See the detailed description in *Dickens at Work*, pp. 93–94.

42. See Needham, "The Undisciplined Heart of David Copperfield," *NCF*, pp. 81–107.

43. The best discussion of the problem is in *Dickens at Work*, pp. 202–21.

THE INSTALLMENT DIVISIONS

I

Divisions Between Installments*

SERIALS WITH FAT INSTALLMENTS[1]									
Installment No.	Chapters Allotted to Individual Installments								
	PP[2]	NN[3]	MC[4]	D & S[5]	DC[6]	BH[7]	LD[8]	OMF[9]	ED[10]
1	1–2 (24 pp.)[2]	1–4	1–3	1–4	1–3	1–4	1–4	1–4	1–5
2	3–5 (24 pp.)[2]	5–7	4–5	5–7	4–6	5–7	5–8	5–7	6–9
3	6–8 (regular 32 pp.)[2]	8–10	6–8	8–10	7–9	8–10	9–11	8–10	10–12
4	9–11	11–14	9–10	11–13	10–12	11–13	12–14	11–13	13–16
5	12–14	15–17	11–12	14–16	13–15	14–16	15–18	14–17	17–20
								Воок II	
6	15–17	18–20	13–15	17–19	16–18	17–19	19–22	1–3	21–23
7	18–20	21–23	16–17	20–22	19–21	20–22	23–25	4–6	
8	21–23	24–26	18–20	23–25	22–24	23–25	26–29	7–10	
9	24–26	27–29	21–23	26–28	25–27	26–29	30–32	11–13	
10	27–28	30–33	24–26	29–31	28–31	30–32	33–36	14–16	
							Воок II	Воок III	
11	29–31	34–36	27–29	32–35	32–34	33–35	1–4	1–4	
12	32–33	37–39	30–32	36–38	35–37	36–38	5–7	5–7	
13	34–36	40–42	33–35	39–41	38–40	39–42	8–11	8–10	
14	37–39	43–45	36–38	42–45	41–43	43–46	12–14	11–14	
15	40–42	46–48	39–41	46–48	44–46	47–49	15–18	15–17	
								Воок IV	
16	43–45	49–51	42–44	49–51	47–50	50–53	19–22	1–4	
17	46–48	52–54	45–47	52–54	51–53	54–56	23–26	5–7	
18	49–51	55–58	48–50	55–57	54–57	57–59	27–29	8–11	
19	52–57	59–65	51–54	58–62	58–64	60–67	30–34	12–17	

* The abbreviations are as follows (the novels are listed in chronological order):

Pickwick Papers	PP	Bleak House	BH
Oliver Twist	OT	Hard Times	HT
Nicholas Nickleby	NN	Little Dorrit	LD
The Old Curiosity Shop	OCS	A Tale of Two Cities	TTC
Barnaby Rudge	BR	Great Expectations	GE
Martin Chuzzlewit	MC	Our Mutual Friend	OMF
Dombey and Son	D & S	Edwin Drood	ED
David Copperfield	DC		

II

Divisions Between Installments

[Dashes, extra numbers, and variations from the regular pattern are explained in the notes to individual novels and indicate oddities in their publication history]

SERIALS WITH LEAN INSTALLMENTS[1]

Chapters Allotted to Individual Installments

Installment Number	OT[11]	OCS[12]	BR[13]	HT[13]	TTC[14]	GE[15]
1	1–2	1 4[12]	1	1–3	1–3	1–2
2	3–4[11]	2	2–3	4–5	4	3–4
3	5–6	3–4 4	4–5 (last 3 of 4)[12]	6	5	5
4	7–8	5	6–7	7–8	6 (end of Bk. I)	6–7
5	9–11 (after lapse)	6–7	8–9	9–10	1–2	8
6	12–13	8	10–11	11–12	3	9–10
7	14–15	9–10	12 4	13–14	4–5	11
8	16–17 (after lapse)	11–12 5	13–14[13]	15–16 (end of Bk. I)	6	12–13
9	18–19	13–14	15–16	1	7–8	14–15
10	20–22 (orig. end of Bk. I)	15–16	17–18	2–3	9	16–17
11	23–25	17–18	19–20	4–5	10–11	18
12	26–27	19–20 4	21–22 5	6	12–13	19
13	28–29 & 30 (orig. 29 & 30 were Ch. 7 of Bk. II)	21–22	23–24	7	14	20–21 (end of 1st stage)
14	31–32	23–24	25–26	8	15	22
15	33–34	25–26	27–28	9–10	16	23–24

II (cont.)

Divisions Between Installments

[Dashes, extra numbers, and variations from the regular pattern are explained in the notes to individual novels and indicate oddities in their publication history]

SERIALS WITH LEAN INSTALLMENTS[1]

Chapters Allotted to Individual Installments

Installment Number	OT[11]	OCS[12]	BR[12]	HT[13]	TTC[14]	GE[15]
16	35–37 (orig. end of Bk. II)	27–28 / 4	29–30 / 4	11–12 (end of Bk. II)	17–18	25–26
17	38–39	29–30	31–32	1–2	19–20	27–28
18	40–41 (after lapse)	31–32	33–34	3–4	21	29
19	42–43	33–34	35–36	5–6	22–23	30–31
20	44–45	35–36	37–38 / 4	7–9	24 (end of Bk. II)	32–33
21	46–49 (orig. 47–48 were Bk. III, Ch. X)	37 / 5	39–40		1	34–35
22	49 cont. –51	38–39	41–42		2–3	36–37
23	51 cont.	40–41	43–44		4–5	38
24	52–53	42–43	45–46		6–7	39
25		44–45 / 4	47–48 / 5		8	40 (end of 2nd stage)
26		46–47	49–50		9	41–42
27		48–49	51–52		10	43–44
28		50–51	53–54		11–12	45–46

II (*cont.*)

Divisions Between Installments

[Dashes, extra numbers, and variations from the regular pattern are explained in the notes to individual novels and indicate oddities in their publication history]

SERIALS WITH LEAN INSTALLMENTS[1]

Chapters Allotted to Individual Installments

Installment Number	OT[11]	OCS[12]	BR[12]	HT[13]	TTC[14]	GE[15]
29		52–53	55–56		13	47–48
30		54–55 ___ 5	57–58 ___ 4		14	49–50
31		56–57	59–60		15	51–52
32		58–59	61–62			53
33		60–61	63–64			54
34		62–63 ___ 4	65–66 ___ 4			55–56
35		64–65	67–68			57
36		66	69–70			58–59
37		67–68	71–72			
38		69–70	73–74			
39		71–72 ___ 5	75–76 ___ 5			
40		73 (1st of 4)[12]	77–78			
41			79–80			
42			81–82 ___ 5			

APPENDIX 2

STOCK CHARACTERS AND INCIDENTS AND MOTIFS

THE FOLLOWING LISTS are not exhaustive, but will indicate to some degree the extent and general nature of Dickens's uses of these devices. Some characters, incidents, or other devices are in more than one category.

We should remember Forster's comparison: Dickens's "greatness," he says, quoting Hazlitt on Shakespeare, "is in distinctions of like characters."[1]

CHARACTERS	NUMBER OF BOOKS	NUMBER OF NAMES
Generally unsympathetic characters:		
Avaricious lawyers	7	11
Wicked businessmen	8	17
Avaricious criminals	7	10
People avaricious in private life	10	17

(Continued overleaf)

CHARACTERS	NUMBER OF BOOKS	NUMBER OF NAMES
Mysterious enemies	7	7
Malicious wrongdoers	11	18
Fanatical "Christians"	8	17 + 1 mob
Other fanatics	13	28 + 1 group
Haughty or useless aristocrats	12	30 + 1 group
Shrewish wives	10	16 + 1 group
Unpleasantly aggressive females	12	27
"Betrayed" women	7	12
People cut off from the world	11	24
Hard, proud people	11	31
Selfish, proud people	8	12
Usually unfortunate and sympathetic characters:		
Women oppressed by male relatives	7	9
Women oppressed by husbands or lovers	12	19
Prisoners	12	25
Impoverished people	12	45 (12 children)
Thoughtless young men	12	15
People incapable of handling money	5	11
Failures	11	22
Childlike characters	10	27
Disfigured or injured (mind or body)	11	31
Wards or orphans	15	37 (5 are male)
Protagonists who are children	11	16 (11 are female)
Older men who are protagonists	9	9
Young women who are merely saintly	9	10
Characters who are powerful and help others (some exceptions):		
Guardians	15	28
Kind old gentlemen who help people	14	32

CHARACTERS	NUMBER OF BOOKS	NUMBER OF NAMES
Eccentric clerks who help people	10	12
Unsuccessful lovers who help people	10	14
Faithful servants who help people	11	15
(33 types; 15 novels)		

EXAMPLES OF CHARACTER TYPES

(× = *exceptions, who are sympathetic or partly so*)

Avaricious lawyers: Dodson, Fogg, Pell, Perker ×, Brass, Spenlow, Vholes, Tulkinghorn, Rugg ×, Stryver, Jaggers ×.

Wicked and avaricious businessmen: Ralph Nickleby, Hawk, Squeers, Gride, Quilp, Tigg, Pecksniff, Heep, Smallweed, Krook, Bounderby, Merdle, Flintwich, Casby, Fledgeby, Wegg, Hexam.

Avaricious criminals: Fagin, Sikes, Dodger, Rudge, Jonas Chuzzlewit, John Carker, Blandois, Compeyson, Riderhood, Radfoot.

People avaricious in private life: Jingle, Trotter, Monks, Mrs. Sliderskew, Bray, Brooker, Snawley, Trent ×, Trent's grandson, Chester, Mrs. Brown, Mrs. Skewton, Murdstone, Skimpole, Dorrit, Mr. and Mrs. Lammle, Boffin (a pretense) ×, Bella ×.

Mysterious enemies: Monks, Rudge, Mrs. Brown, Alice ×, Tulkinghorn, Blandois, Orlick, Jasper.

People whose deeds are largely the result of malice: Monks, Ralph Nickleby, Mrs. Sliderskew, Quilp, Chester, Hugh, Mrs. Brown, Alice ×, Edith ×, Hortense, Mrs. Clennam, Mr. and Mrs. Defarge, Marquis D'Evrémonde, Evrémonde's brother, Orlick, Headstone, Jasper.

Fanatical Christians: Mrs. Weller, Rev. Stiggins, Humm, preacher at Little Bethel, Mrs. Nubbles ×, Gordon, Mrs. Varden, the mob, Mrs. MacStinger, Murdstone, Mrs. Jellyby, Mr. and Mrs. Chadband, Mrs. Snagsby, Mrs. Pardiggle, Quade, Mrs. Clennam, Honeythunder.

Other fanatics: Pott, Slurk, Trent ×, Chester, Martin Chuz-
zlewit, Sr., Anthony Chuzzlewit, Dombey, Carker, Gills
×, Peggotty ×, Wickfield ×, Carstone ×, Miss Flite ×,
Gridley ×, Gradgrind, Bounderby, Dorrit, Blandois,
Mr. X and Mrs. Defarge, Jacques three, "the Venge-
ance," the mob ×, Pip ×, Miss Havisham, Magwitch
×, Betty Higden ×, Podsnap, Veneering, Durdles.

Haughty or useless aristocrats: Mr. and Mrs. Nupkins,
Verisopht, Hawk, Mr. and Mrs. Wititterly, Mr. Man-
talini, Chester, Ruth, Pinch's two employers, Edith
Dombey ×, Mrs. Skewton, Feenix ×, Steerforth's
mother, Steerforth, Dedlock ×, Lady Dedlock ×,
Volumnia, other relatives, Harthouse, Mrs. Merdle,
Sparkler ×, Marquis D'Evrémonde, Evrémonde's
brother, Monseigneur, Miss Havisham, Drummle,
Wrayburn ×, Mortimer ×, Mrs. Tippins, Twemlow ×.

Shrewish wives: Mrs. Pott, Mrs. Weller, Mrs. Nupkins,
Mrs. Bumble, Mrs. Sowerberry, Mrs. Nickleby, Mrs.
Kenwigs, Mrs. Squeers, Mrs. Lillyvick, Mrs. Quilp's
friends, Mrs. Varden, Mrs. Jellyby, Mrs. Snagsby, Mrs.
Clennam, Mrs. Merdle, Mrs. Defarge, Mrs. Gargery,
Mrs. Wilfer.

Other unpleasantly aggressive women: Mrs. Bardell, her
two friends, Mrs. Pott's maid, Miss Knag, Mrs. Quilp's
mother, Sally Brass, Miggs, Pecksniff's two daughters,
Sarah Gamp, Betsy Prig, Mrs. Todgers, Mrs. Pipchin,
Mrs. Blimber, Mrs. MacStinger, David's landlady, Miss
Dartle, Mrs. Markleham, Mrs. Sparsit, Mrs. General,
Fanny, "the Vengeance," Estella, Lavvy, Mrs. Lammle,
Lady Tippins.

"Betrayed" women: Oliver's mother ×, his father's legal
wife, Alice ×, Edith ×, Emily ×, Miss Dartle, Betsey
Trotwood ×, Lady Dedlock ×, Clennam's father's mistress, Mrs. Clennam, Mrs. Defarge's sister, Miss
Havisham.

People who have cut themselves off from the world: Ralph
Nickleby, Newmann Noggs ×, Gride, Madeline Bray
×, Trent ×, Mrs. Rudge ×, Mr. Haredale, Martin
Chuzzlewit, Sr., Dombey, Edith ×, Carker, David's
aunt ×, Wickfield ×, Krook, Lady Dedlock ×, Haw-
don, Mrs. Clennam, Miss Wade, Miss Havisham,
Hexam, Riderhood, Headstone, Rokesmith ×, Jasper,
Neville.

People one of whose main traits is pride and/or the suppression of emotions or lack of emotions which Dickens seems to feel are associated with pride; important characters analyzed with some fullness: Chester, Jonas Chuzzlewit, Dombey, Edith, Murdstone, the Steerforths, Mrs. Clennam, Dorrit, Pip, Estella, Bella, Wrayburn, Jasper; *and the following additional characters:* Ralph Nickleby, Dolly Varden, Heep, Lady Dedlock, George, Tulkinghorn, Hortense, Gradgrind, Bounderby, Tip, Gowan, the Marquis and his brother, Miss Havisham, Magwitch, Orlick, Lavvy, Mrs. Wilfer, Sapsea.

People one of whose main traits is the selfishness Dickens associated with pride: Chester, Gashford, Martin Chuzzlewit, Jr., Mrs. Skewton, Skimpole, Tom Gradgrind, Dorrit, Tip, Fanny, Pip, Charlie Hexam, Sapsea.

(○ = *exceptions, who are unsympathetic*)

Women oppressed by male relatives: Arabella, Nicholas's sister Kate, Nell, Emma Haredale, Florence, Louisa Gradgrind, Little Dorrit, Lizzie Hexam, Miss Podsnap, Pleasant Riderhood.

Women oppressed by husbands or lovers: Nancy, Mrs. Mantalini, Mrs. Quilp, Mrs. Rudge, Dolly Varden, Merry, Edith, the first Mrs. Dombey, David's mother, Agnes, Mrs. Smallweed, brickmason's wife and her friend, Lady Dedlock, Louisa, Mrs. Gradgrind, Pet, Miss Wade, Mrs. Defarge's sister, Lizzie Hexam, Rosa.

Prisoners (or men held by law): Pickwick, Weller, Jingle, Trotter, others, Fagin, Oliver, Squeers, Kit, Barnaby, his father, Hugh, the hangman, others, Jonas Chuzzlewit ○, Micawber, George, Dorrit, Clennam, Cavalletto, Blandois ○, others in Marshalsea, Manette, Darnay, Carton, others, Magwitch, Compeyson, others, Neville.

Impoverished people (children in italics): Oliver, people in workhouse, people in district where Sowerberry goes to measure corpse, especially the widower, Nicholas Nickleby, Sr., his wife, his two grown children, the *boys* at Squeers's school, *Nell*, Trent, stoker, mother of deaf and dumb child, her *child*, her friend, people in manufacturing district, the *"Marchioness,"* Barnaby and his mother, Edith's aunt and cousin, *David*, the Micawbers, *Charley* and *her family*, *Jo*, Hawdon, Miss

Flite, the brickmason and his family and *baby* and friends, Jupe and Sissy, Rachael [*sic*], Stephen, his wife, the workers in Coketown, Maggie, the Dorrits, the prisoners in the Marshalsea, Clennam, the French people as a whole—in St. Antoine and in country village especially—*child* who is run over, her father, Mrs. Defarge's sister, brother, father, brother-in-law, Betty Higden, the *boy* who throws stones.

Thoughtless young men (who get themselves or others into trouble or come close to doing so): Verisopht, Swiveller, Martin Chuzzlewit, Jr., Steerforth ○, Rob the Grinder ○, Carstone, Harthouse, Tom ○, Tip, Gowan, Darnay, Pip, Wrayburn, Edwin Drood, Neville.

People incapable of handling money: Trent, Carstone, George, Mr. Jellby, Skimpole ○, Dora, Micawber, Tom Gradgrind ○, Dorrit ○, Mrs. Clennam ○, Tip ○.

Failures: Noggs, Trent, Haredale, Pecksniff ○, Lewsome, Dombey ○, Gills, Micawber, Miss Trotwood, Wickfield, Carstone, Gridley, Miss Flite, George, Dorrit ○, Merdle ○, Clennam, Mrs. Clennam ○, Pancks, much of business world, Carton, Twemlow, Grewgious's clerk.

Childlike characters: Mrs. Nickleby, Smike, Mrs. Nickleby's lover, Mrs. Sliderskew ○, Trent, Barnaby Rudge, Toots, Cuttle, Dora, Micawber, Mrs. Micawber, Mr. Dick, Wickfield, Skimpole, Miss Flite, Carstone, Flora, Mrs. F's aunt, Mrs. Plornish's father, Maggie, Affery, Dorrit, Dr. Manette, Mrs. Gargery, Mr. Wilfer, the Boffins.

Disfigured or injured people (disfigured mentally or physically): Smike, Mrs. Nickleby's lover, Trent, Nell, Joe, Barnaby, Tappertit, Dombey, Toots, Little Dombey, Miss Dartle, Mr. Dick, Miss Flite, Gridley, Carstone, Krook, Mr. Jellyby, Caddy Jellyby's child, Stephen, his wife, Mrs. Gradgrind, Mr. Jupe, Affery, Mrs. Clennam, Dorrit, Dorrit's brother, Maggie, Dr. Manette, Mrs. Gargery, Miss Havisham, Wrayburn, the dolls' dressmaker.

Ward or orphans (or neglected children); those in italics were "born in sin": Snodgrass, Arabella, Winkle, Oliver, Rosa, others, Nicholas and his sister (for all practical purposes), Smike (for all practical purposes), Nell, Emma Haredale, young Chester (for all practical

purposes), Mary, Martin Chuzzlewit, Jr., Walter,
Toots, Florence (for all practical purposes), David,
Dora, Agnes, *Esther*, Carstone, Ada, Rosa, Sissy and
others (for all practical purposes), Clennam, Tatty-
coram, Miss Wade, Little Dorrit (in a way), Lucie,
Carton, Pip, Estella, John Harmon, Bella, *Sloppy*,
Johnny, Lizzie and Charlie Hexam (for all practical
purposes), Edwin Drood, Rosa.

*Protagonists who are children for at least a while at the
start of the book (hero and heroine of every book
which has a hero and heroine):* Oliver, Nell, Walter,
Florence, David, Agnes, Esther, Sissy, Louisa Gradgrind, Little Dorrit, Lucie, Pip, Estella, Edwin Drood,
Rosa, Neville, Neville's sister.

*Mature or older men who are protagonists or extremely im-
portant characters (○ here signifies those who are not
sympathized with or are not unfortunate):* Pickwick
○, Trent, Haredale, Dombey ○, Jarndyce (the guardian) ○, Stephen, Clennam, Carton ○, Crisparkle ○.

*Young women who are merely saints—i.e., have no other
character or purpose:* Madeline, Nell, Mary, Florence,
Agnes, Esther, Ada, Sissy, Little Dorrit (most of the
time), Lucie.

*Characters who are powerful and help others—exceptions
who do not help are marked⊗:* Guardians: Pickwick,
Benjamin Allen⊗, Brownlow, Mrs. Maylie, Ralph
Nickleby⊗, others (in NN)⊗, Trent⊗, Haredale, Martin Chuzzlewit, Sr., Gills, Mr. Wickfield, Miss Trotwood, Murdstone⊗, Jarndyce, the court of Chancery⊗,
Gradgrind, Little Dorrit (in a way), Mrs. Clennam⊗,
Meagles, Mr. Lorry, the Gargerys, Jaggers, Miss Hav-
isham⊗, Mr. and Mrs. Boffin, Betty Higden, Honey-
thunder⊗, Jasper, Crisparkle.

Kind old gentlemen who help people: Pickwick, Wardle,
Brownlow, his friend Grimwig, Losberne, the two
Cheeryble brothers, Crummles, Garland, Trent's
brother, the schoolmaster, Garland's brother, the
vintner, Varden, Martin Chuzzlewit, Sr., Gills, Cuttle,
Feenix, Wickfield, Micawber, Jarndyce, Boythorn,
Meagles, Dr. Manette, Mr. Lorry, Jaggers, Boffin,
Twemlow, Riah, Crisparkle, Tartar, Grewgious.

Eccentric clerks who help people: Perker's clerk, Newman

Noggs, Tim Linkinwater, Swiveller, Chuffey, Pinch, John Carker, Micawber, Guppy, Pancks, Wemmick, Bazzard.

Unsuccessful lovers who help their ladies or their ladies' friends or relatives: Sawyer, Verisopht, Swiveller, Kit, Joe, young Haredale, Pinch, Toots, Ham, Jarndyce, Boythorn, Woodcourt, Chivery, Carton.

Faithful servants who help people (mainly by encouraging them): Weller, Mr. Brownlow's housekeeper, Kit, the "Marchioness," John Grueby, Mark Tapley, Nipper, Peggotty, Mrs. Roundtree, Phil (the gypsy), Sissy Jupe, Little Dorrit, Maggie, Cruncher, Miss Pross.

A few other character types I have not listed. For instance, there are the following:

Usually unsympathetic nuisances: easily flattered, silly women—spongers.

Sympathetic: eccentric understudies—helpers; saucy boys—helpers; innocents—helped.

Still I believe I have listed most of the examples of the main types. The major characters who do *not* fit in any of the above categories or who are not merely the husbands of shrewish wives or the wives of oppressive husbands may be listed very briefly: Tupman, Harry, Miss LaCreevy, Browdie, Kit's sweetheart, Willet, Sr., Westlock, Dr. Strong, Creekle, *Bucket,* Bagnet, Doyce, turnkey, Sparkler, Herbert Pocket, Mrs. Venus, Mortimer, *Datchery,* Crisparkle's mother (18 characters in 12 books).

From some points of view, the lists of stock incidents and situations below could be called lists of motifs, images, or symbols, as could the prior lists of characters.[2] They also are obviously not exhaustive, but may indicate certain Dickensian preoccupations.

	Books	*People*
Attempts at seduction	6	7
Love affairs where there is opposition	9	10
Romeo and Juliet love affairs	5	6

Queer environments for children	9	22
Schools	11	20
Love affairs where one party delays	8	11
Marriages unhappy because loveless	14	28
People driven by fear	11	16
Murder	9	14
Love affairs between older men and young women	6	10
Odd love affairs	8	12
Love affairs without real opposition	7	8
Deaths of children	7	9
Deaths	15	79
People whose pride is softened or beaten down	15	51
Letters telling all	4	6

To get down to cases and names, let us look at the following list.

Attempts at seduction: Kate Nickleby, Dolly, Emma Haredale, Edith, Louisa, Lizzie, Rosa Budd.

Love affairs where there is opposition from girl's parent or guardian: Arabella, Madeline, Emma, Mary Graham, Dora, Ada, Caddy, Pet, Estella, Bella (a pretense).

Romeo and Juliet love affairs: Young Chester and Emma Haredale, Clennam and Little Dorrit, Gowan and Pet, Lucie and Darnay, Lizzie and Wrayburn, Edwin and Helena Landless.

Queer environments for children: the workhouse, Fagin's, the curiosity shop, the carnival people, the factories, the church and graveyard, Murdstone household, Peggotty's, Creakles' school, Jellyby household, Gradgrind household, circus people, the Marshalsea, Miss Havisham's household, Gargery household, the Drood betrothal.

Schools: PP, NN, OCS, MC, D & S, DC, BH, HT, GE, OMF, ED.

Love affairs where one party delays: Miss Maylie, Kate, Nicholas, Madeline, Dolly, David (*in re* Agnes), Esther (*in re* Woodcourt), Clennam, Estella, Bella, Wrayburn.

Marriages unhappy because loveless (those threatened

only are italicized): Mr. and Mrs. Weller, Sr., *Jingle and Miss Wardle, Pickwick and Mrs. Bardell, Sawyer and Arabella,* Oliver's father and his legal wife, Mr. and Mrs. Bumble, Mr. and Mrs. Mantalini, *Madeline and Gride,* Mr. and Mrs. Lillyvick, *Swiveller and Nell, Gashford and Emma Haredale, Tappertit and Dolly Varden,* Mr. Chester and his wife, those of Pecksniff's two daughters, Dombey's second marriage, Mrs. MacStinger's second marriage, David's mother and Murdstone, *Jarndyce and Esther,* Lady Dedlock and Sir Leicester, Louisa and Bounderby, Mr. and Mrs. Clennam, Gowan and Pet, *Mr. Dorrit and Mrs. General,* Sparkler and Fanny, Estella and Drummle, *Lizzie and Headstone,* Mr. and Mrs. Lammle, *Rosa and Edwin, Rosa and Jasper.*

People driven by fear (whose emotions Dickens shows the reader): Winkle, Sikes, Trent, Nell, Rudge, Jonas, Carker, Lady Dedlock, Esther, Bucket, Darnay, Pip, Magwitch, Headstone, Betty Higden, Rosa.

Murders: (by) Sikes, Rudge, mob, Jonas, Hortense, Rigaud, Gaspard, Marquis's brother, mob, Orlick, Jaggers's maid, Headstone, unknown murderer of Radfoot, Rider and Radfoot (in near-murder of Harmon), Jasper (probably).

Love affairs between older men and young women: Oliver's parents, Gride and Madeline, Jarndyce and Esther, Lady Dedlock and Sir Leicester, Bounderby and Louisa, Stephen and Rachael, Clennam and Little Dorrit, Clennam and Pet, Crisparkle and Helena, Tartar and Rosa.

Odd love affairs: Mr. and Mrs. Bumble, Lillyvick and Miss Petowker, Mrs. Nickleby and the madman, Tim and Miss LaCreevy, Swiveller and Sally Brass, Swiveller and the "Marchioness," Tappertit and Dolly, Traddles and his fiancée, Guppy and Esther, Chivery and Little Dorrit, Lavvy and Sampson, Fledgeby and Miss Podsnap, Venus and Pleasant Riderhood (!).

Love affairs without real opposition: Snodgrass and Wardle's daughter, Kit and Barbara, Westlock and Ruth, Walter and Florence, Richard and Ada, Jarndyce and Esther, Lucie and Darnay, Edwin and Helena Landless.

Deaths: Mrs. Weller, prisoner in Fleet, little Dick, Oliver's mother, the woman measured for coffin, Nancy, Sikes, Sikes's dog, Fagin, Verisopht, Nicholas's father, Ralph, Gride, Nell, Trent, Quilp, the schoolmaster's friend, Rudge, Emma's father, Willet, Chester, Hugh, Dennis, Barnaby, the blindman, others in *BR*, Tigg, Jonas, Anthony, Paul, Mrs. Skewton, Carker, Alice, David's father and mother, Ham, Steerforth, Barkis, Jo, Lady Dedlock, Hawdon, Carstone, Krook, Tulkinghorn, Hortense, Esther's aunt, Gridley, Jenny's baby, Bounderby, Stephen, Mrs. Gradgrind, Mr. and Mrs. Clennam, the two Dorrit brothers, Merdle, the turnkey, Blandois, Pet's sister, Rigaud's wife, Carton, seamstress, Marquis, Marquis's murderer, murderer's child, Mrs. Defarge, others in *TTC*, Mrs. Gargery, Miss Havisham, Pip's parents, Compeyson, Magwitch, Headstone, Riderhood, Hexam, Radfoot, Harmon (almost), Johnny, Betty Higden, Jenny's father, Edwin, Jasper, (and thus especially *OT, BR, BH, LD, TTC, OMF*).

People whose pride is softened or beaten down: Dowler, Jingle, Trotter, Stiggins, Monks, Bumble, Sikes, Squeers, Ralph Nickleby, Hawk, Mrs. Nickleby, Trent, Brass, Tappertit, *Mrs. Varden*, Dolly, Willet, *Haredale*, Pecksniff, *Martin the younger*, Dombey, Edith, Edith's cousin, Carker, Steerforth's mother, Em'ly, Lady Dedlock, Lord Dedlock, Carstone, Mrs. Jellyby, Mrs. Snagsby, Gradgrind, Louisa, Harthouse, Clennam, Dorrit, Mrs. Clennam, Tip, Monseigneur, others, Pip, Estella, Miss Havisham, Mrs. Gargery, Bella, Wrayburn, Headstone, Veneering, Lammles, Fledgeby, Edwin Drood, Neville, Jasper (according to plans).

Letters telling all: Edith, Lady Dedlock, Jarndyce, Miss Wade, Mrs. Clennam, Dr. Manette.

All the tables suggest an obsession with the maltreatment of passive sympathetic characters, but I am afraid that this method is not trustworthy about details. At every point—in the selection of categories, definition of categories, classification of individual details, selection of individual details, memory of the materials, interpretation of the results—this method involves an unusual amount of subjectivity. Yet its results are too cut and dried. So the reader must judge whether the general patterns indicated by such studies agree with his own knowledge of the works and discount the details. For these reasons I do not think that an exhaustive study of Dickens's imagery or motifs or plot devices or names or anything else of that kind can possibly be conclusive or worthwhile. I believe that the general patterns are significant; the reader must judge for himself whether they are consistent with the other evidence in this book.

Certain overall plot patterns are plainly visible, and consistent with the *general* patterns noted above. *Oliver Twist, Nicholas Nickleby, Martin Chuzzlewit, David Copperfield, Our Mutual Friend,* and, to a lesser extent, *The Old Curiosity Shop, Dombey and Son,* and possibly *Edwin Drood,* are about young men who make good despite the opposition of usually criminal personal enemies who are punished in the end. Perhaps *Great Expectations* belongs to this group. *Bleak House, Little Dorrit, Our Mutual Friend, Dombey and Son, Martin Chuzzlewit,* and probably *Edwin Drood* and *Hard Times,* are to some extent about virtuous women who eventually get the men and financial position they deserve. The opposition is usually more in the nature of misfortune than villainy. In other words, twelve of the fifteen novels involve the idea of a young person's coming into his own, and the reader is carried through incident after incident because of his identificaton of himself with a young character and his sense that this character is despite all the plot complications somehow gradually growing toward a golden destiny. *Barnaby Rudge* and *A Tale of Two Cites,* the two historical novels, have no real heroes, but many protagonists and antagonists. Both involve mobs and mob action and destructive mob emotion a good deal. *The Old Curios-*

ity Shop and *Hard Times* are alike in being about girls
whose lives are wrecked by their relations' stupidity.
Pickwick Papers, Dickens's first novel, stands alone
thematically. We can say then that almost all Dickens's novels are variations of the Cinderella story, for
almost all of Dickens's heroes and heroines reach
happiness because of the energetic help of outside
forces, as in *Our Mutual Friend.*

There is evidence that Dickens *thought* in these
motifs and that his thought was repetitive, using the
same counters many times. In connection with *A Tale
of Two Cities* there are references (undated) in a list of
titles in the memoranda book[3] which suggest the development of his ideas in this and other books to some
extent. Mr. Ley comments:

> It will be seen that *Our Mutual Friend* was thought of
> as a possible title for the book that preceded it by some
> years. *Somebody's Luggage* and *No Thoroughfare*, ulti-
> mately used as titles for Chirstmas stories, were also
> potential titles for the book which for so long was *Nobody's
> Fault*, but in the end became *Little Dorrit*. We have *Mem-
> ory Carton*, which suggests that the idea of *A Tale of Two
> Cities* was already in mind. *Rokesmith's Forge* is interest-
> ing, too. No doubt here is the idea that shaped itself into
> Joe Gargery's forge, though the name found its way into
> one book and the forge into another—neither of them the
> book for which he was seeking a title. *Dust* certainly hints
> at *Our Mutual Friend.*[4]

Similar repetitions and overlappings of names and
motifs are pointed out by Jackson and Lindsay,[5] and
one can see for oneself that such titles as *Rokesmith's
Forge* involve a combination once in Dickens's mind of
ideas later separate in his books. The very process of
thinking about a whole string of names when trying to
start a novel, testified to by Forster on many occasions,

indicates a kind of obsessive or repetitive movement of mind, in which one re-plows and re-plows an area of subject matter until a clear story line is seen. This movement produces, in the long run, stories with certain repeated or redistributed elements.

APPENDIX 3

THE INSTALLMENT PATTERNS

Example of pattern (a): (several incidents from several plot lines). The sixteenth installment of *Martin Chuzzlewit*:

Chapter XLII. Carriage turned over—Jonas Chuzzlewit tries to get horses to trample Tigg—another man saves Tigg—it all appears innocent—Bailey almost dead—they put up at an inn—Jonas Chuzzlewit is in Tigg's room in the morning—Tigg decides to return alone when he goes back.

Chapter XLIII. Tapley reunited with Mrs. Lupin—she tells Martin Chuzzlewit and Tapley the news about Martin's grandfather—Tapley advises Martin Chuzzlewit to make up with Martin Chuzzlewit, Sr.— Pecksniff tears up Martin Chuzzlewit's letter—Martin

Chuzzlewit and Tapley force their way into the house—Martin Chuzzlewit asks for forgiveness and for work, no more—Martin Chuzzlewit, Sr., tells Martin Chuzzlewit, Jr., to go away—Mary admires Martin Chuzzlewit's conduct—says Pecksniff's suit is not pushed by Martin Chuzzlewit, Sr.—they pass Jonas Chuzzlewit as they leave Pecksniff's.

Chapter XLIV. Jonas Chuzzlewit persuades Pecksniff that Tigg has a good thing—Pecksniff plans to settle this finally two days later at Salisbury—Jonas Chuzzlewit goes.

Example of pattern (b): (several suitable incidents from one plot thread of which the last was a curtain because it was last). The tenth installment of *Nicholas Nickleby*:

Chapter XXX. Miss Snevellicci flirts with Nicholas—she has him to a party to meet her parents—Mr. Lillyvick falls on Mr. Snevellicci—Nicholas leaves party—a London manager appears—another letter from Noggs.

Chapter XXXI. Ralph Nickleby shows signs of affection for Kate—Noggs threatens Ralph Nickleby, who is not present, at Miss La Creevy's and tells her about Kate and how he has sent for Nicholas—afraid Nicholas will be rash if he hears news at once—they plan to be out.

Chapter XXXII. Nicholas arrives—leaves Smike at Nogg's—goes off—overhears Hawk talk of his sister—learns all—asks Hawk's name—refused—strikes Hawk—carriage which Hawk is in smashed—Nicholas leaves almost stunned.

Chapter XXXIII. Nicholas goes back to Nogg's—next morning Nicholas takes Kate away from her employers—they take their mother to Miss La Creevy's—she is told all—Nicholas sends Ralph Nickleby a letter—Ralph reads it.

Examples of pattern (c): (the parts of an installment in a pattern with a slow beginning, a middle building up to something, and a climactic end). Dickens frequently used this pattern for his installments. Sometimes he used a single plot thread in this third pattern (c_1—see below) but he often used several (c_2), merely increasing his pace as he proceeded. The tenth installment of *Dombey and Son* and the eighteenth of *Little Dorrit* are examples of c_1 and c_2 respectively.

Installment 10, *Dombey and Son*

Chapter XXIX. Miss Tox hears (at her house) Mrs. Chick's news that Dombey is to be married again—she faints—Mrs. Chick quarrels with her and breaks off her friendship.

Chapter XXX. Edith comes to Florence, is friendly—asks her to promise to come home as soon as wedding trip begins no matter who invites her elsewhere—Edith makes her mother agree not to keep Florence after wedding—forgives her mother for this match, hopes God forgives her—spends the night by Florence's bed.

Chapter XXXI. Dombey's wedding.

Installment 18, *Little Dorrit*

Chapter XXVII. John's father asks Clennam not

to mind John—John continues to be kind, but not shake hands and to speak in a hostile way—refuses to say why—John has Clennam to tea—speaks of his love of Little Dorrit, asks him why he does not speak freely—finally tells Clennam Little Dorrit loves Clennam—Clennam, surprised, goes back to his cell and thinks—Plornishes visit him.

Chapter XXVIII. Clennam makes no friends—his health declines—one of the Barnacles visits him—is glad Circumlocution Office has not put Clennam where he is—tells him to forget the invention—Rugg fails to persuade Clennam to change prisons—Blandois appears, followed by Cavalletto and Pancks—Clennam asks Blandois what his purpose in casting suspicion of murder on his mother is—Blandois demands wine—Blandois explains he was blackmailing Clennam's mother and she was too stubborn, so he has scared her—he laughs at exposure—says no one will expose him—writes a letter to Mrs. Clennam giving her a week—Blandois taunts Clennam—Pancks brings Flintwich who hands Clennam a note from his mother saying to mind his own business—Flintwich tells Blandois Mrs. Clennam accepts his terms—they go—Pancks promises to see it through.

Chapter XXIX. Clennam sick—Little Dorrit comes—she says her brother has come home to see to her father's will—asks Clennam to take all her money—he refuses—she leaves—John Chivery comes to say Little Dorrit sends Clennam her love—shakes Clennam's hand.

Example of pattern (d): (the inclusion of a *surprising* sensational incident from one plot thread at the end of an installment which has had incidents from several plot threads—none of which has been as sensational as the final, surprising one). The tenth installment of *Bleak House:*

Chapter XXX. Mrs. Woodcourt distresses Esther by talk of her son's fickleness—Caddy's wedding.

Chapter XXXI. Jo sick at brickmaker's—he thinks Esther is lady who gave him money—he is brought to Bleak House—he is gone in morning—Charley and Esther get sick.

Chapter XXXII. Guppy and Jobling (alias Weevle) wait for the time Krook is going to hand over Hawdon's letters—grease all over the place—they find Krook gone, but signs of a burnt body.

The seventh installment of *Barnaby Rudge*, the fifteenth of *The Old Curiosity Shop,* and the fourth of *Hard Times* are examples of patterns *e, f,* and *g,* respectively.

Installment 7, *Barnaby Rudge*

Chapter XII. Chester and Haredale agree to break up Edward and Emma's romance by subterfuge.

Installment 15, *The Old Curiosity Shop*

Chapter XXV. The schoolmaster holds school, but lets the boys go at noon—Nell and he visit the sick boy—who dies.

Chapter XXVI. Nell and Trent leave the schoolmaster and are taken in by the lady with the caravan.

Installment 4, *Hard Times*

Chapter VII. Mrs. Sparsit—Gradgrind takes Sissy from Bounderby's house (where she spent a night).

Chapter VIII. Tom talks to Louisa—says she will enable him to stay in favor with Bounderby.

The following table gives the number of some installments which are further examples of each type. Appendix 1 lists the chapters in each installment of each of Dickens's novels. The reader, by using that list, can ascertain for himself the use of these patterns.

The number of examples in any one book of any one kind is not indicated above. I did notice two facts of interest, however, as I prepared this table. In *David Copperfield*, David is brought into every chapter, and one point of view is maintained constantly. So types a, c_1, and d are not found in *David Copperfield*. And in *Great Expectations*, Dickens's last weekly serial, an extraordinary number of installments follow pattern e. I think that installment patterns c_2 and e are the hardest of the patterns to execute; e obviously is frequently like c_2 in effect.

Pickwick Papers tends not to use the regular installment patterns until after the first half of the book; installments 1, 2, 4, 5, 6, 7, 8, 9, 10, 11, 16, and 19 (naturally this last) end softly or have an ordinary incident at the end. They have their most interesting incidents at the beginning or the middle. Perhaps this fact is partly responsible for the extraordinarily rapid pace of *Pickwick Papers*—especially its first nine installments. Apparently Dickens developed his regular patterns in the last half of *Pickwick Papers*, for *Pickwick Papers* 3, 14, 18 are c_1; *Pickwick Papers* 12, 13, 17 are a; *Pickwick Papers* 15 is b; and then Dickens used these patterns in all his later books.

Monthly Installment Patterns	Book	Installment
a	NN	5, 7, 11
	D & S	4, 7, 14
	BH	3
	LD	2, 6, 12, 16
	ED	3
b	MC	6
	DC	8, 18
c_1*	MC	17
	D & S	15
	BH	5, 15
	ED	5
c_2	DC	4, 10
	BH	18
d†	MC	14
	LD	1
e	OCS	1, 6
	HT	3, 9
	TTC	6, 20
	GE	3, 5, 18, 24, 33, 34
f	OT	7
	OCS	7, 20
	BR	2, 17, 37
	HT	10, 14
	TTC	10, 13
	GE	9, 12, 31
g	OT	8, 9
	OCS	9, 29
	BR	10, 18
	HT	2
	TTC	7, 8
	GE	15

* c_1 is especially easy, because Dickens shifts from one plot to another and then to a third and fourth and can arrange the bits of his plots in any order he chooses.
† d is easy to execute for the same reasons c_1 is.

Incidentally, on rare occasions the serials with leaner installments had one of the monthly installment patterns. Thus *A Tale of Two Cities* 26 is c_1 and *Great Expectations* 26 is *b*. This tendency is especially true of *Oliver Twist,* which was published monthly, but which occasionally lapsed for a month and had an unusually large installment the month after each lapse as the reader can see from the Appendix 1 chapter list II and Note 11 to that list. For example, *Oliver Twist* 5 and 10 are c_2, and *Oliver Twist* 13 is *a*.

Lastly we notice the fact that Dickens uses *curtains* in almost all his installments—but not necessarily sensational ones. On rare occasions he uses a "manufactured" curtain.[1] The end of Chapter XLV of *The Old Curiosity Shop* is one. Nell shrieks and faints as she suddenly sees the face of a gentleman to whom she has gone to ask for help. The beginning of the next chapter (and of the next installment) reveals that this gentleman is her old friend the schoolmaster. The reader has been misled. Nell instead of being terrified at the sight of some new danger is actually happy.

The installments to which Dickens paid most attention were the smallest in which the story appeared. *The Old Curiosity Shop* and *Barnaby Rudge,* which appeared simultaneously as weeklies, monthlies (approximately), and bound volumes are constructed as weeklies, though a faint monthly pattern is apparent. *A Tale of Two Cities,* which appeared in simultaneous weekly and monthly parts, is similarly constructed.[2]

Yet some attention was given to larger units. *Hard Times,* though a weekly serial, was planned in the larger serial portions. Mr. Butt and Mrs. Tillotson say that the fact was indicated "at the head of the first number plan."[3] *Oliver Twist* had been divided in three "books" originally.[4] There were in other early books great watershed events without formal marking which had produced a vague but wide change: Pickwick's going to prison, the end of the first half of *Barnaby Rudge,* Paul Dombey's death and Dombey's marriage,

David's running away from London and his marriage. They divide the books roughly into halves or thirds. "From *Hard Times* onwards," say Mr. Butt and Mrs. Tillotson, "each novel, except for *Edwin Drood,* is divided into books even in serial issues."[5]

APPENDIX 4

A DESCRIPTIVE BIBLIOGRAPHY
OF WORKS WITH IMPORTANT THEORIES
ABOUT STORY AND THE NOVEL

As FAR as I have been able to discover, there is no history of the theory of fiction. The list below is only a subjective selection, but long miscellaneous lists of undescribed works about the novel are available elsewhere. The descriptions here emphasize the special quality of the individual critic and overlap less than the works described do. I have limited the entries to those which seem original and might help one learn how to write a story, especially a novel, by defining what one is trying to do.

I. Works emphasizing the reaction of the audience:
    a. Edmund Burke—*A Philosophical Inquiry Into the Origins of Our Ideas of the Sublime and the Beautiful* (1756)
        We call beautiful something which is

small, orderly, significant. The sublime is caused by fear, which is in turn aroused by vast size, infinite number, obscurity, incompleteness. This work had a tremendous effect on Gothic, sensational, and Transcendentalist writers because it suggested that vigorous emotional and physical reactions are produced by vividly contrasted stimuli. There is no satisfactory discussion of the meaning and impact of this work.

b. William Hazlitt—Miscellaneous essays

Writers should dramatize, not state. They should suggest, not supply completeness. They should use an informal style. Writing should combine sense of material fact, emotion, and idea. Objects are captured by artists when they respond to them personally and identify themselves with them and penetrate to their essences. Humor is caused by incongruity. These views influenced Keats, Dickens, Thackeray, probably Hardy, possibly James, T. S. Eliot, and others and encouraged the sensational tendency of Anglo-American fiction. Most of them are drawn, often indirectly, from Schiller, Kant, Coleridge, lesser Scottish critics. There is almost no discussion of Hazlitt's work. The best selection of the theoretical essays and a good discussion are in W. J. Bate, *Criticism: The Major Texts* (New York, 1952). Influences upon Hazlitt and Hazlitt's reading and early thought are discussed very helpfully in Herschel Baker's *William Hazlitt* (Cambridge, Mass., 1962).

c. *Natyaçastra*—A Hindu work of perhaps 300 A.D.—primarily a discussion of drama and related matters such as the dance.

The drama produces eight basic moods. In the skillful evocation and variation of these lies the art. These moods, however, are different from responses to real stimuli, for all are related aspects of an esthetic response. Since to the Hindus drama traditionally was the best of literature, and since the Hindus most valued an art which combined semi-realistic representation, dynamic rhythm, and some idealization of subject, this work promoted the use of plot, dance, and language for an effect akin to a vision of the ideal. It expresses a general, lyrical view of story which is common in the Orient and an idea of art which anticipates Kant and F. Schlegel. Goethe knew the dramas of Kalidasa which followed its principles. Possibly the work was known to the German Romantic writers generally. For discussion of the work itself, see A. B. Keith, *Sanskrit Drama* (1924).

d. *Tractatus Coislinianus* (anonymous)

A classical fragment on comedy suggesting that the incongruous and exaggerated cause laughter. Some humorous devices are listed. A translation and discussion are available in Lane Cooper, *An Aristotelian Theory of Comedy* (New York, 1922).

e. Seami (or Zeami) Motokiyo—Critical essays about the No plays—*c.* 1400

The No (or Noh) play's chief effect should be wonder. This is achieved by strange, ghostly subjects and by the actor's exerting such control that his appearance and actions, even normally ugly ones, appear beautiful to the audience at all times. The actor's mind must unify all his devices to maintain power over the audience. The play should ultimately have the effect of being still and unmoving. Here again, in the theory of the great developer of the No plays, there occurs the Oriental tendency toward a lyric use of story. Excerpts in translation are available in Donald Keene, *Anthology of Japanese Literature* (London, 1956).

f. Chikamatsu Monzaemon—Comments on the puppet theatre reported by a friend—in *Naniwa Miyage* (1738) by Hozumi Ikan

Composition is aimed at arousing emotion. It is good when a drama has one overall mood or can be dominated by one situation. Pleasing entertainment is a mixture of the unreal and real; so dialogue needs stylization. Externally unrealistic things may be said, as by women or villains or clowns, to express real inner feelings of characters. Even descriptions must be full of emotion, but the emotion to be aroused should not be announced. Instead it should be stimulated by indirect details. Here the greatest of Japan's dramatists seems to make more of plot than Zeami, but for emotional effect mainly. Available in translation in Donald Keene, *Anthology of Japanese Literature* (London, 1956).

g. Faubion Bowers—"The Esthetics of Kabuki," *Japanese Theatre* (London, 1954)

The Japanese consider drama the combination of all arts. The goal of spectacular effect upon the audience unifies the various parts of Kabuki. Since the Japanese have written little about their theatre, this book is that rare thing— a profound study of fresh material. Again we must note the primarily lyrical rather than dynamic use of story.

II. Works emphasizing the reality represented:

a. Plato—*Ion*

The traditional Greek view of the Homeric epics is that they contain all wisdom and knowledge, that art is to teach. Is the artist not mad, though? How can he teach? This work is thus a source of the idea that art is to teach, of the idea that the artist is an inspired madman, and of a doubt about the helpfulness of art.

b. Jeremy Collier—*A Short View of the Immorality and Profaneness of the English Stage* (1698)

Poetic justice ought to govern the drama because the audience will believe and imitate what it sees on the stage. This author took up the old idea that art should serve the world which it pictured by teaching morality and described devices by which this service could be performed in story. His rule was disobeyed by few English novels before 1845. Economically and politically propagandist novels have used the same principle to this day (the "good" or approved are shown rewarded at the end of the story; the "unsound" or "bad" are shown "punished").

c. Euripides—*Electra*

Forms, even traditional ones, if without content, are dangerous lies. Literature should be realistic.

d. Plato—*Republic,* Book X

Poetry (here epic and tragedy) is a false, moving imitation of a reality of static essences. Ever since the *Republic,* there have been those, like Thackeray and George Eliot, who have had a basic suspicion of the forms and patterns of story.

e. Stendhal—*The Red and the Black* (1830)

The author is a "passenger." He carries "a mirror along the roadway." This is one beginning of the French doctrine that the author should be detached from the world and story he pictured (the very opposite of the English Hazlit-

tian passionate observer). Flaubert elaborates
the theory in some of his letters. Taine and Zola
develop it into a "scientific" coolness.

f. Émile Zola—*The Experimental Novel* (1800)
    "The observer in him [the novelist] gives
the facts as he has observed them, fixes the
point of departure, establishes the solid ground
on which characters are going to walk and
phenomena develop. Then the experimentor
prepares and sets up the experience, that is to
say, causes the people to move in a specific
story to show that the succession of facts will be
what the nature of the studied facts will force."
His vision was of a naturalistic (or scientific) de-
terministic story developing one idea. In this
story what he felt were the established principles
of heredity, environmental influence, and psychology would be shown operating in a selected,
arranged body of material. His own vivid, tightly organized, sensational, semi-dramatic novels
persuaded several generations that a novel
should develop a single theme and that the ugly
was true. Yet obviously Zola's love of shocking
his audience distorted the world pictured in his
books, and his fine artistic selection of detail and
his symbolism contradicted his notions of open-
minded scientific observation.

g. Plato—*Symposium*
    Abstract essences (or forms, ideals, ab-
solutes) of things exist. By loving one beautiful
object, then others, one can pass to an awareness of the beauty of all things, to the idea of
beauty itself, and to a life in contact with the
ideal, including absolute truth and goodness as
well as beauty. Applied to sexual love by the
Arab world and Renaissance Europe, this gen-

eral view was reapplied to people in general and to objects in landscape by the cult of sensibility, as in Shaftesbury's *Characteristics* and Wordsworth's poems. In practice it meant that the writer by creating attractive pictures could improve and enlighten the reader.

h. Wordsworth—Preface to *Lyrical Ballads* (1800)

The poet has looked steadily at his subject and avoided traditionally elegant phrasing. He has selected simple country people because human emotions are found in more ideal form among such. He has chosen common events, colored them by imagination, and made them "interesting by tracing in them . . . the primary laws of our nature." Pleasure leads our minds; so the poet must give pleasure at once. A similar purpose was expressed by Dickens who said in a speech about the time of *Oliver Twist* that he had tried to find the "soul of goodness" put even in evil things by God. In this aspect of their work both these writers tried to discover the wonderful and ideal in ordinary people and events and to make it beautiful. This principle, the idealism of Hegel and others, and the idea of Novalis's blue flower in his unfinished novel *Heinrich von Ofterdingen*, in which a poet seeks to make the world into a dream, persuaded generations to accept once again the platonic view that the ideal and beautiful was the true, that the pretty and pleasant and eventually the merely customary were art. Zola and World War I demolished this faith, but only after it had supported many Victorian happy endings. Wordsworth's and Dickens's search for the ideal among common people also raised the stature of the novel, which had always pictured such persons more than most other genres.

i. Horace Walpole—Preface to the second edition of *The Castle of Otranto*

The realistic journalistic novelists are omitting a part of reality. In leaving the supernatural out of their books, they neglect the imagination of man. This novel was widely read. The preface is a revolutionary manifesto heralding the appearance of the Gothic novel tradition, which developed in imitation of *The Castle of Otranto* (1764). Walpole said he wished to fuse the romance and the novel.

j. E. M. Forster—*Aspects of the Novel* (1927)

E. M. Forster is captivated by Bergson's vision of an organic stream of life and consciousness opposed by the divisions, boxes, and artificial re-connections to which reason and mechanical science have reduced life. He decries plot and device as mechanical and neat and exalts a rather shapeless spontaneity. He condemns an esthetic pattern organized around some one idea (James's ideal) and calls for a composition which is more a rhythm, waxing and waning. He laments the fragments of people we see in life and says that the glory of the novel is its ability to show us whole characters intimately. He attacks one-principle characters as flat and calls for "rounded" characters which can surprise us believably (because they are complex, whole people). He discusses many other aspects of the novel also. Despite his interest in rather formless rhythm, Forster's emphasis is essentially on the problem of representing realities. Like other critics of this kind, his theory is dominated by his definition of reality.

k. Friedrich Schiller—*On Simple and Sentimental Poetry* (1795)

The simple or naïve literature of the classics was social in orientation, concrete, objective, balanced. The literature of the modern world is private, abstract, subjective, sentimental, distorted. This theory is one of the greatest attempts to relate ancient literature to modern. Essentially the reality to be captured in art is seen as ruling the author and determining the form of the art.

l. Ian Watt—*The Rise of the Novel* (Berkeley, 1957)

England in the eighteenth century was a new individualistic society dominated by the middle class. The novel was the characteristic literary expression of this new age and reflected the individual's interest in feeling, romance, reality, economics, and many other specific things. One of the best definitions of the novel in this century, this book nevertheless has trouble accounting for Fielding and Smollett, whose lives and books were not primarily internal or economic.

m. G. W. F. Hegel—*Lectures on Aesthetics* (delivered in 1818)

Tragedy is the reconciliation of two great moral forces in conflict. For a discussion see R. Wellek, *A History of Modern Criticism*, Vol. II; and A. C. Bradley's lecture "Hegel's Theory of Tragedy." In more general form this idea had been important to the Greeks, who spoke of *protagonist* and *antagonist*. It has also been important in modern readings of the novel.

Surprisingly, this important principle is not mentioned by Aristotle nor usually mentioned in connection with the problems of constructing a fiction (for an exception, see Cleanth Brooks and Robert Penn Warren, *Understanding Fiction*, Appendix). The idea is based on Hegel's theory of conflict in the universe and in the process of knowing.

III.   Works emphasizing the artist:

a. Laurence Sterne—*Tristram Shandy* (1760–1767)

In mottos, direct comments, and procedures, Sterne states and implies clearly a theory of the novel. The meanings of actions, not actions themselves, are said to be important. The meanings of actions are shown to lie in mental associations. Both actions and associations are shown to be nearly chaotic and organized by each individual subjectively. The book itself is declared to be such a subjective toy of the author's. Thus the conventional novel's tight structure based on a plot composed of external actions is inappropriate to the nature of authorship and personality. This book expanded the horizons of the novel and pushed it, especially in Germany, toward a more lyrical pattern.

b. Friedrich Schlegel—"Letter on the Novel," *Gespräch über die Poesie* (1800)

The novel includes all other genres. It is ironic and romantic. It is subjective and modern, the very type of the modern "sentimental" literature opposed by Schiller to objective classicism. It results from the free play of the creating imagination. It is a personal, sometimes fantastic, reflection of the author.

This has been a widely influential theory

of the novel. It rationalized the individualism, the loose structure, and the lyrical, nearly plotless approach of Sterne and Richter. It encouraged the sprawling, symbolic procedure of the German novel. In time it offered a rationale for the novels of Joyce and Virginia Woolf. For discussion, see René Wellek, *A History of Modern Criticism*, Vol. II (New Haven, 1955); H. E. Hugo, "An Examination of F. Schlegel's *Gespräch über die Poesie*," *Monatschefte*, XI (1948), 221–31; and A. E. Lussky, *Tieck's Romantic Irony* (Chapel Hill, 1932).

c. Immanuel Kant—*Critique of Judgment* (1790)

Man's response to a beautiful work of art is not moral, practical, or philosophic, nor a matter of personal pleasure, but a reaction to arrangement, an ideal, esthetic response to a universal value. Art is the disinterested organic creation of the imagination working with materials from experience but unrestrained by the chains of involvement in mundane reality. This work is one of the bases of the modern elevation of the artist into a saint and of the modern tendency to distinguish between sincere (and often academic and dull) art on the one hand and commercial (audience-oriented) art on the other. The basic principle became, in time, an influence upon the art-for-art's-sake movement, upon the cult of authorial detachment, and upon that kind of literary criticism which defiantly considers individual works in isolation. Undoubtedly, also, this view of art became combined with the organic theory—popularized by Kant and Herder—that the work of art, the psyche, society, and the universe were like plants. The combination contributed to the appearance of that peculiarly German kind of novel, the

Bildungsroman with its meandering plot; abstract, internal, and intellectualized biographical subject; and symbolic events. For a discussion, see Roy Pascal, *The German Novel* (Toronto, 1956). Like other German Romantics, Kant believed art fused the sensuous and the abstract. This idea is behind many of the pressures to dramatize and symbolize in later literary theory.

d. Joseph Frank—"Spatial Form in Modern Literature," *Criticism: The Foundations of Modern Literary Judgment*, eds. M. Schorer, J. Miles, and G. McKenzie (New York, 1948)

This essay suggests that modern literature tends toward spatial not temporal organization. The novel is seen as becoming less organized around plot and more lyrical. Frank sees Lessing as the originator of criticism of the arts in terms of perception of space and time and mentions recent German writers who use this approach. This work is the best known of recent studies of lyric fiction.

e. Ralph Freedman—*The Lyrical Novel* (Princeton, 1963)

One kind of modern novel is moving away from the devices of story and toward those of the lyric poem. The origins of this development are to be found in the German Romantic writers. In this type of novel, the narrator is a disguise for the author, who presents his inner self as the world of the novel and reveals his attempt to absorb the world into himself. Thus Freedman exposes the subjective concern which is one basis for the lyrical use of story.

f. Georges Poulet—*The Interior Distance*, trans. by Elliott Coleman (Baltimore, 1959)

A series of existentialist critics have been

studying a different pattern. The artist is seen as discovering his identity in the art of expressing himself, as creating himself in the very act of creating a book. His behavior and the behavior of his characters are seen within time and moving through time. One of the most widely known of the works of these critics, Poulet's book analyzes the views of time in a series of works in the French tradition. The work of art as seen by such men who attempt to capture an author's world-view also is largely autobiographical. Hence critics of this kind are very interested in the novel which happens to be mainly a biographical narrative centered on one free personality, often a *Bildungsroman*. One cannot help suspecting that with all their sense of existence and crisis the existentialists are trapped by their acceptance of most of the Kantian view of the mind as a virtually free spatial organizer in an atomized world. The result would seem to be a new cult of the sensual but shapeless lyrical novel in France as opposed to the old German cult of the metaphysical but shapeless lyrical novel. Apparently the literary work emphasizing plot depends upon a firm conviction that reality has some shape. The latest theory in France appears to be Alain Robbe-Grillet's notion of a structure to a novel eventually discovered by its author after a beginning like some lyric poets' in words, rhythms, etc. In Dickens studies, Poulet's most distinguished follower is J. Hillis Miller, *Charles Dickens: The World of His Novels* (1958). Dicken's love of spontaneity and his poetic tendencies make his work very fruitful ground for such criticism, though critics of this kind overlook

Dickens's equally fine sense of structure and mechanics. Miller is also the author of one of the best discussions of Poulet, "The Literary Criticism of Georges Poulet," *Modern Language Notes*, 78 (December, 1963), 471–88. Miller notes the spatial quality of Poulet's view of time.

IV. Works emphasizing the artistic product itself:

a. Giraldi Cintio (or Cinthio)—*Discorso intorno al comporre dei Romanzi* (1549)

Aristotle's ideas do not apply to the romance, a new genre unknown in his day. Moreover, Tuscan language and spirit are different from the Greek; so Tuscan literature should have its own principles. There are two kinds of romances. The better kind tells of the actions of many men and is fiction. An inferior kind treats of the many actions of one man, is historical, and should start at the beginning of his story. For discussion, see J. E. Spingarn, *History of Literary Criticism in the Renaissance* (New York, 1924) and C. S. Baldwin, *Renaissance Literary Theory and Practice* (New York, 1939).

b. William Congreve—*Preface to Incognita* (1692)

Romances deal with miraculous and impossible and exotic events. Novels deal with the usual and familiar. The two types had been known in Renaissance Italy. Congreve put the distinction into words. It reappears in critical writing throughout the last 275 years.

c. Boris Tomashevsky—*Teoriya literatury* (Leningrad, 1931)

Plot is different from structure, which is the arrangement and distortion of plot. A brief explanation of this idea of one of the leading Russian formalists may be found in R. Wellek and

A. Warren, *A Theory of Literature* (New York, 1956), Chapter 16.

d.   I. A. Richards—*Practical Criticism* (London, 1929)

The problem of understanding poetry and literature is largely to be overcome by careful study of the individual texts. This book is the chief modern source of the New Criticism, whose principal method has been to apply German Romantic views of the organic nature of art to particular works. August Schlegel, Coleridge, and Hazlitt had used this approach on Shakespeare's plays. They tended to see the central seed as a main character. Modern use of the method tends to find a central action or a central metaphor or device.

e.   Cleanth Brooks and Robert Penn Warren— *Understanding Fiction* (New York, 1959)

About 1940 the application of the New Criticism to fiction became much more common. This book applies the method systematically. The character of the assumptions involved is made clear in its Appendix, which summarizes the principles felt by the authors to be involved in composing fiction (here short stories). The authors display an interest in setting and in conflict.

f.   Edwin Muir—*The Structure of the Novel* (1929)

Muir describes several kinds of novel. His most interesting emphasizes space and character, has a loose plot ranging over a broad area, and is roughly parallel to comedy. Another kind has a tight plot emphasizing causality and a final resolution; it is built on a time principle; it is rather dramatic and parallel to tragedy. Some of Muir's observations are important, but his work is limited by his purpose—primarily classification. Also, some of his ideas, like the proposition that temporal novels make more of relationships than do spatial ones, are patently false.

V. Works and critics combining the interests in audience or public, in reality or problem exterior to the product, in author, and in the artistic product itself thus achieving an integrated architectural sense of the creation:

a. Aristophanes—Parabasis of *The Clouds*
Good art is original.
—Parabasis of *The Birds*
Fun is good for the health.
—*Thesmophoriazusae*

Literary art imitates its subject, involves the identification of the author with his characters and the expression of himself. Work which is exaggerated and melodramatic is bad. Moreover, art full of improper ideas may corrupt the public.

—*The Frogs*

The parts of a drama should be related to the whole. The devices are projections of the subject. There are accepted rules for composing dramas.

b. Aristotle—*Poetics*

The *Poetics* itself seems almost a summary of a longer work. Its ideas have been frequently applied to the novel. Some of the more important are indicated here. Art imitates nature. There are several modes of imitation. Tragedy is the ideal story. The essence of story is plot, which may be equated with plot outline. Character is revealed by choices. Thought, diction, music, and spectacle are less important elements of tragedy. The best plot combines an appearance of chance reversal with a recognizable causal pattern. The best tragic hero is a man of mixed quality. He should pass from good fortune to bad because, though primarily good, he has done something wrong. Tragedy arouses pity and fear. Wish-fulfilling poetic justice and the ugly are inherent in comedy. These and simply hundreds of other ideas, all of them full of suggestion for the writer, have made the *Poetics* for centuries the *sine qua non* of story criticism. Unfortunately, some of the principles are not useful in forms of story which have many aspects beside plot or which are lyrical in tendency. Furthermore, Aristotle is least interested in the talent of the individual artist. In the Renaissance, Italian critics applied his theory of tragedy to the epic. This "epic" theory was later applied by Fielding to the novel.

c. Henry Fielding—Preface to *Joseph Andrews* (1742)

The source of humor is the exposure of affectation. The novel is a comic epic in prose.

—*Tom Jones* (1749)

Contrast and the use of foils are inherent in all beauty. The novel is an entertainment for the audience. What is provided is human nature itself. In life virtue is not necessarily a prelude to good fortune (in theory, Fielding saw weaknesses in Collier's call for didactic poetic justice). He regretted that the world frowns on "all historical writers who do not draw their materials from records." The author should be able to see the essences of things he observes and to distinguish between them, especially between like characters.

d. August Schlegel—Essays and lectures

Plato in his *Phaedo* had seen myth as an imaginative exploration of possibility. Kant in his *Critique of Pure Reason* had seen the symbol as the basic tool by which imagination made knowing possible by organizing the many phenomena so that they could fit into twelve categories and become part of the unity of consciousness. Eighteenth-century theories about the development of language had stressed that it was metaphoric in nature. August Schlegel popularized the obvious corollary of all these ideas, namely that literature is symbolic. Moreover, in line with the views of many of the German Romantics, he held that the symbols in literature reflected the organic concentrics of life and of the universe itself. From the wide influence of this view came both a new sense of how to organize a novel and a feeling for the interrelation of audience, author, reality represented, and artistic product. From it have come also the Romantic and modern failure to see that often symbols act as merely mechanical complexities which obscure rather than as magic or automatic transmitters of reality. Hence come, then, those many-volumed, endlessly complex German novels whose only claim is infinite seriousness in the tireless repetition of moral clichés. Eventually the French poets and modern novelists of many nations tried these ideas. For discussion of the ideas of A. Schlegel, see R. Wellek, *A History of Modern Criticism,* Vol. II.

e. C. G. Jung—Miscellaneous works (see below)
      Schiller, Dilthey, and other German thinkers had suggested that there were various types of human beings. Freud had developed a

psychology which described types of abnormal
personalities. Jung developed a system of his
own which attempted to describe ordinary behavior types. Much of it is a reworking of Schiller's and Kant's systems. The universe is ultimately unknowable. The mind, however, has a
level of experience, the collective unconscious,
full of the past and the experience of the race.
By means of metaphors, called archetypes by
Jung, the many materials of experience are
made recognizable and unified for the conscious
mind. The basic mental operations are seen as
full of opposites, which are fused by the mind,
which seeks unity and relates the past to the
present conditions of life in order to resolve the
imbalances and conflicts of the individual's present life. Jung saw the artist as using archetypal
images expressing concepts from the collective
unconscious to suggest to his age what it needed
for unity in itself and unity with past and for the
prevention of mass neurosis. Jung distinguished between introverts and extroverts. He
described four basic functions of the mind—
thinking, feeling, sensation, and intuition. He
made extensive studies of dreams and archetypal literary motifs, which he related to the
different operations of the mind in the relations
described above. In consequence, Jung's own
ideas have broad implications in regard to the
audience of literature and the reality represented in it as well as in regard to the structure
of the work itself and the personality of the
author. Indeed, Jung's thought tends to tie these
subjects together in meaningful patterns. Hunt-
ing down Jungian archetypal patterns in literature of all kinds has seemed a weird sport to the

uninitiated, but its point has been to identify what Jungian critics believe are the cures prescribed by individual artists for their eras. The best summary of Jung's thought, a book approved by Jung himself, is Jolande Jacobi, *The Psychology of C. G. Jung* (New Haven, 1964).

f. N. Frye—*The Anatomy of Criticism* (Princeton, 1957)

Frye describes four basic kinds of narrative fiction. His most important distinctions are between the social, extroverted novel and the symbolic, introverted romance and between these forms, which emphasize people, and others which emphasize ideas in purer form. Frye is interesting as one example of what can be done with Jungian ideas.

g. H. James—*The Art of the Novel*, ed. R. P. Blackmur; *The House of Fiction*, ed. Leon Edel

James's criticism is striking not for its novelty so much as for its reasonable syntheses of most earlier ideas about story. His criticism is marked by its sensitive interrelating of the simultaneous solutions of art's many problems and, in his prefaces, its long discussions of his own methods. He talked of architecture frequently because that idea fused the mechanical and organic for him. It also fused audience and artist and the given problems of reality. Among James's particular interests might be said to be dramatic procedure, the presentation of materials through the lens of an interesting character's mind, organic development from a central idea. Always concerned with morality, but horrified at the clumsiness and lecturing of moral English novelists, James came to combine Hazlitt's involved artist and the French detached author, the English grasp of personality and the French sense of slick form. For discussion, see Blackmur's introduction to *The Art of the Novel,* R. Wellek, *A History of Modern Criticism,* Vol. IV, and J. A. Ward, "James's Idea of Structure," *PMLA,* LXXX, No. 4, part 1 (Sept., 1965), 419–26.

h. W. C. Booth—*The Rhetoric of Fiction* (Chicago, 1961)

Using James against the Jamesians like Perry Lubbock (in *The Craft of Fiction*), Booth denies that fiction should always be dramatic or that it can ever be wholly detached. Fiction has many tools which are used in different combinations on different occasions. Implicitly an author always seeks to persuade readers to accept his world-view and uses fiction as the rhetoric to persuade. Booth explores in great detail the use of various points of view as devices to present this or that view. The book is made less good by its tendency in the last two-thirds to equate all the rhetoric of fiction with points of view, but this study is full of possibilities and has articulated the widespread dissatisfaction since 1945 with Lubbock. This study also marks the ultimate in the modern rejection of the ancient distinction, explicit in Aristotle, between rhetoric with its primarily intellectual, even logical, sequence and poetic (including story) with its primarily emotional and imaginative sequence. For a discussion of this distinction, see C. S. Baldwin, *Ancient Rhetoric and Poetic* (New York, 1924), pp. 1–5.

NOTES TO APPENDICES

Appendix 1

THE INSTALLMENT DIVISIONS

1. The text has explained the distinction.
2. T. Hatton and S. Cleaver, *A Bibliography of the Periodical Works of Charles Dickens* (London, 1933), p. 3. Publication lasted from Apr., 1836, to Nov., 1837, except for June, 1837. The indications of the numbers of the chapters in each installment come from the following pages of *Periodical Works of Dickens:* 35, 37, 40, 42, 45, 47, 49, 52, 60, 61, 64, 71, 75, 76, 80, 84, 88. The reader can see that the contents of each installment are hardly indicated clearly in *Periodical Works of Dickens.* Much other information useful to a *book collector* is, however. Each number was independent—a little magazine as it were, with its own advertising. It cost a shilling.
3. *Periodical Works of Dickens*, p. 131. Publication lasted from Apr., 1838, to Oct., 1839. Chapter numbers in individual installments (hereafter referred to merely as "chapter numbers") from *Periodical Works of Dickens*, pp. 137–44, 146–49, 151–52, 154–57, 159.
4. *Periodical Works of Dickens*, p. 185. Publication lasted from Jan., 1843, to July, 1844. Chapter numbers from *Periodical Works of Dickens*, pp. 190–93, 195–200, 202–3, 205–8, 210–11.
5. *Periodical Works of Dickens*, p. 227. Publication lasted from Oct., 1846, to Apr., 1848. Chapter numbers from *Periodical Works of Dickens*, pp. 230, 232–35, 237–38, 240–48, 250.

See also Kathleen Tillotson, *Novels of the Eighteen-Forties* (Oxford, 1956), Appendix III, p. 318.

6. *Periodical Works of Dickens*, p. 253. Publication lasted from May, 1849, to Nov., 1850. Chapter numbers from *Periodical Works of Dickens*, pp. 256–72.

7. *Periodical Works of Dickens*, p. 275. Publication lasted from Mar., 1852, to Sept., 1853. Chapter numbers from *Periodical Works of Dickens*, pp. 281–82, 284–87, 289–91, 293–96, 298–302, 304.

8. *Periodical Works of Dickens*, p. 307. Publication lasted from Dec., 1855, to June, 1857. Chapter numbers from *Periodical Works of Dickens*, pp. 312–30.

9. *Periodical Works of Dickens*, p. 345. Publication lasted from May, 1864, to Nov., 1865. Chapter numbers from *Periodical Works of Dickens*, pp. 350–55, 357, 359–61, 363–70.

10. *Periodical Works of Dickens*, p. 373. Publication lasted from Apr., 1870, to Sept., 1870. Dickens had *died* on June 9, 1870. He devoted great attention to this work, but never told the end. The last issue cost 1/6. Chapter numbers from *Periodical Works of Dickens*, pp. 376–77, 379, 381–82, 384.

11. Bentley's *Miscellany* (London, 1837), Vol. I–II; 1838, Vol. III–IV; 1839, Vol. V. Publication was as follows:

Year	Month	Installment Number
1837	February	1
	March	2
	April	3
	May	4
	June	none
1837	July	5
	August	6
	September	7
	October	none
	November	8
	December	9
1838	January	10
	February	11
	March	12
	April	13
	May	14
	June	15
	July	16
	August	17
	September	none

	October	18
	November	19
	December	20
1839	January	21
	February	22
	March	23
	April	24
Total:		24 installments

Dickens says on p. 1 of the Preface to "Collier's Unabridged Edition" that the magazine version was *not quite complete.* This statement is not in the Gadshill edition. I have found only a few minor differences. For instance, on the first page (108) of the first serial edition, Oliver's birthplace is called *Mudfog,* a name Dickens, the editor of the *Miscellany,* uses in other stories before and after this first issue. The end of the first installment (p. 115) refers to more installments and says that the author will not tell whether the story will be long or short—unlike Dickens's later practice (see Note 13). The original chapter divisions and markings were somewhat different from the ones in modern editions. They are indicated on the installment table. The first two installments were only about 10½–12 pages out of an average issue of the *Miscellany* of about 108 pages. They gradually grow until the average in the last third of the novel is 16 pages out of 104–8 pages of the issue of the *Miscellany.* The *second* serial publication of *Oliver Twist* was in ten *equal* parts and the main information on *this* publication comes from *Periodical Works of Dickens,* p. 215. This second publication lasted from Jan., 1846, to Oct., 1846 (almost a decade after the first serial publication). The chapter numbers on this second serial edition, whose divisions are indicated by single lines on the summary, come from the following pages of *Periodical Works of Dickens:* pp. 218–24. The second serial edition's divisions obviously have no significance except insofar as they indicate Dickens's ability to *divide* an already written novel. The last of these divisions of the second edition is a conjecture of mine. *Periodical Works of Dickens* states that it comes within Chapter "LX" (see *Periodical Works of Dickens,* p. 224), but this must be a misprint. The book ends with LIII, and such a large installment is unlikely anyway except as a final installment. I have not been able to find a copy of this edition, so I am assuming that Dickens divided the same chapter in both editions, namely Chapter XLIX.

12. Charles Dickens, *Master Humphrey's Clock* (London, 1840), Vol. 1 and (1841) Vols. 2 and 3—an edition, which, as the Library of Congress file card on it says, is "in the original parts and numbers," but which requires considerable study before one can find the divisions. It is the source of the divisions of the weekly installments. The page numbers check with those referred to in *Periodical Works of Dickens.* This

book was published in three ways at once, weekly installments, approximately monthly installments (formed by binding the *texts* of 4 or 5 of the independent weekly installments together—see *Periodical Works of Dickens*, p. 163), and bound volumes (three of them). Publication began on April 4, 1840, and lasted until Nov. 27, 1841 (*Periodical Works of Dickens*, 163, and Grubb, "Dickens' Pattern of Weekly Serialization," *ELH*, p. 141, Note 1). Each weekly installment had twelve pages of text and cost 3*d* (*Periodical Works of Dickens*, p. 163). In the first few installments and in a few places in later ones the *Master Humphrey's Clock* material is brought in (*Periodical Works of Dickens*, pp. 166–68, 175), but Dickens soon settles down to telling the stories of *The Old Curiosity Shop* and *Barnaby Rudge*. The numbers added to the installment summaries of *The Old Curiosity Shop* and *Barnaby Rudge* indicate the number of weekly installments in the approximately monthly installments, which are indicated by *single* lines. The ends of the three volumes are indicated by *double* lines. The information on where the approximately monthly installments of the two novels end is from *Periodical Works of Dickens*, pp. 166–71, 173–80, 182. *The Old Curiosity Shop* ended in the 46th weekly issue. The eleventh approximately monthly part (see *Periodical Works of Dickens*, p. 175) and the second bound volume include both the ending of the former novel and the beginning of the latter.

13. *Household Words,* Charles Dickens, ed. (London, 1854), Vol. IX, Nos. 210 through 229, Apr. 1, 1854–Aug. 12, 1854. About 5 ¼ pages of story appeared in each number (of 24 pages). Volume IX, p. 140, the last page of the number before *Hard Times* began, announces the start of *Hard Times* in the next issue and predicts that it will be *finished* in five months (the prediction is correct—compare with Note 11 and discussion of first installment of the original serial publication of *Oliver Twist*). The price (2*d*) appears on each number.

14. *All the Year Round* [successor to *Household Words*], Charles Dickens, ed. (London, 1859), Vol. I (Apr. 30, 1859–Oct. 22, 1859) and 1860, Vol. II (Oct. 29, 1859–Apr. 7, 1860). *A Tale of Two Cities* appears in Nos. 1 through 31, Apr. 30, 1859–Nov. 26, 1859. About 4½ pages of story appeared in each number (of 24 pages). The first issue advertises simultaneous monthly publication of the novel—*starting* the *next* month. The last item on p. 24 of the first issue of *All the Year Round* (and of *A Tale of Two Cities*) is the advertisement, which says that "next month" the first monthly issue of *A Tale of Two Cities* will appear and that the book will be completed in eight monthly issues (counting the last as two). The price (2*d*) appears on each number. The single lines in the summary indicate the *monthly* divisions. The information on them comes from *Periodical Works of Dickens*. They were published from July, 1859 [the advertisement above apparently was wrong— also apparently one month saw the publication of two installments] to Dec., 1859 (*Periodical Works of Dickens*, p. 333). The

information on the chapters included in the individual monthly installments comes from *Periodical Works of Dickens,* pp. 336–42.

15. *All the Year Round,* Charles Dickens, ed. (London, 1861), Vols. IV and V, Nos. 84 through 119, Dec. 1, 1860–Aug. 3, 1861. About five pages of story appeared in each number (of 24 pages). The last number before *Great Expectations* began advertised its beginning in the next number and *predicted* (correctly) that it would be finished in August (see notes above on *Oliver Twist* and *Hard Times*). The price (2*d*) appears on each number. Detailed plot outlines, installment by installment, may be found in a microfilmed thesis, *Serialization in the Novels of Charles Dickens,* by A. C. Coolidge, Jr. (obtainable through University Microfilms, Ann Arbor, Michigan).

Appendix 2
STOCK CHARACTERS AND
INCIDENTS AND MOTIFS

1. Forster's remark may be found in John Forster's *The Life of Charles Dickens,* ed. J. W. T. Ley (New York [no date]), p. 727. Hazlitt was echoing a remark of Fielding's in Chapter 1, Book X, of *Tom Jones.*

2. The reader will find descriptions and examples of many, many more incidents and situations in Dickens's stories in Jack Lindsay, *Charles Dickens, A Biographical and Critical Study* (New York, 1950). They seem consistent with the general pattern I describe. See also J. Hillis Miller's *Charles Dickens: The World of His Novels* (Cambridge, Mass., 1958), which further describes the pattern of Dickens's symbolism.

3. Ley, Note 478, Forster, pp. 759–60.

4. Ley, Note 478, Forster, p. 760.

5. T. A. Jackson, *Charles Dickens: The Progress of a Radical* (London, 1937), pp. 172–73; Lindsay, pp. 327, 360, 361, 372, 381.

Appendix 3
INSTALLMENT PATTERNS

1. The term is used in M. Joseph and M. Cumberland, *How to Write Serial Fiction* (New York, 1928), pp. 22, 77.

2. Dickens, when he wrote his novels, had to write them in such a way that the smallest or the original installments would sell. So he *created* his novels primarily with the smallest or original installments in mind. Dickens split some novels into formal parts: *Oliver Twist* and *A Tale of Two Cities* and *Great Expectations* into 3; *Little Dorrit* into 2. In the last two,

the split actually represents divisions in the plot. As a matter of fact, Dickens all his life wrote to fill mechanically determined spaces. His articles in the newspapers all average about 1 ⅛ columns. The monthly novel installments were 32 pages. The weeklies were about 5. We can see (from materials in the notes to the chapter diagrams of *Hard Times* and *Great Expectations* in Appendix 1) that Dickens could predict when his stories would be finished. The number of installments in one of his novels generally is a rough multiple of 20, though *Great Expectations* is 36. The number of chapters in one of his novels is generally a rough multiple of 12 or 15 or both, and is usually about 60. Perhaps these extraordinarily rigid artificial numbers helped him keep his sprawling plots together; or perhaps they necessitated the sprawling plots. *Great Expectations*, at any rate, does not suffer from the mechanically determined number of installments. The artificial balancing of motifs in *Our Mutual Friend* is related to this numerically schematic construction in that it also is imposed from without (the story).

3. John Butt and Kathleen Tillotson, *Dickens at Work* (Fair Lawn, New Jersey, 1958), p. 202. A detailed discussion is given the matter on pp. 202–4 of *Dickens at Work*.

4. See Appendix 1.

5. *Dickens at Work*, p. 205.

Index

saw *Dombey and Son* as a soup, 5; advised dramatization and vividness, 5; on his revival of serial, 49, 117; on an installment's requiring a day's thought, 50; his concern for individual installments, 50; his letters more about meanings than his notes, 50; aversion to reworking an idea, 50; speaks of an idea at the heart of each of nine novels, 61; on his search for meaning in farce, 66; favored clear, moral aim in melodrama, 66; *vs.* Cruikshank for using fairy tales to spread his own opinions, 66; said Christmas Books to have effects like morality plays, 66; aware serial encourages overemphasis on the installment, 68; felt serial reader might overlook unity of book, 68; on need for focus on installment and total in *Pickwick,* 90; on *Pickwick's* character and incident without ingenuity of plot, 90; reader to get sense of progression in *Pickwick* as total, 90; on plot as string of beads, 90; has three moves for three installments in mind, 90–91; on trying to emphasize total more than installment, 92; unwillingness to have medium suppress idea, 96; defense of plot alternation as lifelike, 100–101; defense of curtains and packing, 100–101; defense of Fool in *King Lear,* 101; on power of curiosity and suspense, 108; on truth as stranger than fiction, 108; on human appetite for sensation, 108; on offshoots and meanderings of plots, 115; on strength of basic idea and character in

Dombey and Son, 115, 146; on characters in *Dombey and Son* as stock of soup, 116; on writer as weaver, 116–17; on coincidence as fate, 135–36; on development of character during a serial, 146; on building from character, 146; on character as stock of soup, 146; on opening out of hidden sides of character during writing, 147; on difficulty of ending Fagin because so real, 147; on his tendency to comic analogies, 148; on story of *Chimes* dragging him where it wanted, 148; on contrast of grotesque and innocent in *The Old Curiosity Shop,* 150; on surprise at others' quick decisions about his characters, 154; on serial's prevention of connection, 157; on many passages depending on relation to others, 157; on *A Tale of Two Cities* as picturesque, 163; on characters in *A Tale of Two Cities* as swept by event, 163; on seeking the ideal in the ordinary, 216

——Serial arrangement techniques of Dickens: novels written as published, 49–50; planned as published, 50; little planning, 50–51; evidence of general plans for books, 50-51; his notes were lists, 50; notes show he devoted much effort to arrangement, 50–51; packing of installments, 51–52; description of lean installment, 51; description of monthly installment, 51, 231*n*2; multiple plots, 52–53; use of stock characters and incidents, 53–55; list of stock character types, 53; eccentricities to disguise

Stein's wish to avoid plot, 74

Forster, John, biographer of Dickens: his inclusion of many remarks by Dickens, viii; given a general plan of *Edwin Drood*, 51; on Christmas Books as morally and socially symbolic reworkings of children's stories, 65; his much imitated description of the thorough connectedness of *Bleak House*, 68–69; suggested ending of *The Old Curiosity Shop*, 92; discovered manuscript of extra scene for *Edwin Drood*, 116; organic symbolic criticism of Dickens, 174n8 (of Chap. 1)

Frank, Joseph, 175n3

Frankenstein, novel by Mary Shelley: pictures a monster created by science, 27; male, Faustian, supernatural, 150

Freud, Sigmund, 227–28

Friar Bacon and Friar Bungay, 28

Frogs, The, 225

Frozen Deep, The, a play by Dickens and Wilkie Collins: symbolic nature of, 66–67; association children and symbolism, 67

Frye, Northrop, 13, 229

Gaskell, Mrs. Elizabeth: Dickens against an analytic novel by her, 139; her relations with Dickens, who published some of her work, 174n15–175

Gawaine and the Green Knight, Sir, 28

German Novel, The, 221

Gilgamesh, The Epic of, 29, 30

Goethe, von, J. W., 212

Great Expectations: a loose end in, 94; rescue motif

cast away, 170; mentioned, 33, 51, 54, 99, 100, 115, 135, 154, 156, 158, 163, 166, 198, 207

——Achievement: subtle development of single problem, 30; a theme of folly of hope as a way of life, 62; Dickens's world view and technique made to seem natural by child's point of view, 167; fusion of all Dickens's serial techniques in, 167–71; the journey of life, 168; suggestion of sensibility balanced by selfishness, 168–69; analysis central, 169–70; development steady, 170

——Serialization: declared idea at core, 61; halted and redirected before publication, 92; changed ending, 93; switched from monthly to lean weekly installment unit, 116; use of hardest installment pattern, 206; description of an installment of, 235n15; Dickens predicted when it would end, 235n15

Hajji Baba of Ispahan, novel by James Morier, 63–64

Hall, William, publisher of *Pickwick*, 46

Hamlet, 28

Harbage, Alfred, 43

Hard Times: dedicated to Carlyle, 63; contains reforms of villain and victim, 167; mentioned, 31, 51, 54, 61, 115, 154, 158, 198, 199, 234n13

——Failure: unsureness of symbol and structure, 93; lack of analysis of subject, 140–41; analysis and demonstration lagging behind symbolic assertion, 160;

Perception:
———Theories of (*Cont.*)
ence parallel to theoretical process of knowing described by Kant, 83; theory of relativity adapts some of Kant, 128; shortcomings of view of time as one-dimensional, 128–29

———Total movement or interaction perception: ignorance of closeness and externality when involved in complex events, 119; orientation of interaction of self with world sought, 119–24; focus of conflict, internal continuity, points of cleavage in time together form solution, 120–24; events resolutions of conflicts, 122; resolutions by splitting and reorganizing opposing force, 122; individual's tendency to seek human and psychological sequence for inner continuity, 124; complexity of time consistent with space-time continuum, 128; interaction, partnership, simultaneous events more consistent with relativity than study of things in selves, 128–29

Persians, The, 34

Phaedo, 227

Philaster, 28

Philosophical Inquiry, A . . . (of the Sublime and the Beautiful), 210–11

Pickwick Papers: built around innocent crusader in world of humbug, 61; Dickens came to think less of it, 171; stands alone thematically, 199; mentioned, 106, 107, 158

———Serialization: invitation write it from Chapman and Hall, 46; 1847 preface claims Dickens rediscovered serial by accident, 49; events of third installment, 51–52; 1837 preface on double focus upon installment and total, 90; 1837 preface favored progression visible when read as whole, 90; 1847 preface on character and incident without ingenuity of plot, 90; 1847 preface on a plot as a string of beads, 90; begun as serial before novel seen in it, 91; second half more serious, 92; first half does not use regular installment patterns, 206; development of regular installment patterns in second half, 206

Pilgrim's Progress: road metaphor in, 10, 27; everything helps or hinders journey, 30; progression in man's relation to environment and force behind it, 78

Plato's criticism, 213–14, 215–16, 227

Plot outlines, installment by installment, on microfilm, 235*n*15

Poe, E. A., 109

Poetics, The, summary of chief ideas about story, 225–26

Polarity with a progression: sharp polarity a feature of the novel, 29–32; four common types, 30–31; novelist shows organizations in movement, 70; as orientation of reader in time, 71, 74–75; succession of pages suggests movement, 74; speed and surprise needed for full sense of progression, 75; unsuccessful substitutes for progression, 75; partnerships as well as antagonisms in novel usually, 78; lovers and antagonists usually related, 78; progression usually in relation to beloved or to environment, 78; minor characters' rela-